Test Bank

to accompany

McWhorter

Guide to College Reading, 6/e

Jeanne Jones

Longman

New York Boston San Francisco
London Toronto Sydney Tokyo Singapore Madrid
Mexico City Munich Paris Cape Town Hong Kong Montreal

Test Bank to accompany McWhorter, *Guide to College Reading, 6/e*

Copyright ©2003 Pearson Education, Inc.
Publishing as Longman Publishers.

ISBN: 0-321-08865-4

2 3 4 5 6 7 8 9 10-DPC-05 04 03 02

CONTENTS

Introduction

Part One: Chapter Review Quizzes

Set A

Chapter 1 1
Chapter 2 3
Chapter 3 5
Chapter 4 7
Chapter 5 9
Chapter 6 11
Chapter 7 13
Chapter 8 15
Chapter 9 17
Chapter 10 19
Chapter 11 21
Chapter 12 23
Chapter 13 25
Chapter 14 27
Answer Key to Chapter Review Quizzes – Set A 29

Set B

Chapter 1 33
Chapter 2 35
Chapter 3 37
Chapter 4 39
Chapter 5 41
Chapter 6 43
Chapter 7 45
Chapter 8 47
Chapter 9 49
Chapter 10 51
Chapter 11 53
Chapter 12 55
Chapter 13 57
Chapter 14 59
Answer Key to Chapter Review Quizzes – Set B 61

Part Two: Practice Tests

Set A

Chapter 1 65
Chapter 2 67
Chapter 3 69
Chapter 4 71
Chapter 5 73
Chapter 6 75
Chapter 7 77
Chapter 8 79
Chapter 9 81
Chapter 10 83
Chapter 11 85
Chapter 12 87

Chapter 13 89
Chapter 14 91
Answer Key to Practice Tests – Set A 93

Set B
Chapter 1 97
Chapter 2 99
Chapter 3 101
Chapter 4 103
Chapter 5 105
Chapter 6 107
Chapter 7 109
Chapter 8 111
Chapter 9 113
Chapter 10 115
Chapter 11 117
Chapter 12 119
Chapter 13 123
Chapter 14 125
Answer Key to Practice Tests – Set B 127

Part Three: Vocabulary Quizzes
Quiz 1... 131
Quiz 2... 133
Quiz 3... 135
Quiz 4... 137
Quiz 5... 139
Quiz 6... 141
Quiz 7... 143
Quiz 8... 145
Quiz 9... 147
Quiz 10 149
Answer Key to Vocabulary Quizzes 151

Part Four: Final Exam 155
Answer Key to Final Exam.. 163

Bibliography 165

INTRODUCTION

This assessment package contains two types of assessment for each chapter in *Guide to College Reading*: chapter review quizzes and practice tests. These alternative measurements provide the instructor with a variety of opportunities to assess students' ability to learn and apply techniques and strategies presented in the text. This package also includes ten vocabulary quizzes and a final exam consisting of selected questions from the chapter review quizzes.

CHAPTER REVIEW QUIZZES

The chapter review quizzes are primarily intended to provide an assessment of students' knowledge and comprehension of chapter content.

There are two sets of chapter review quizzes. Each set includes a ten-item multiple-choice quiz for each chapter. Although the concepts tested in each set are similar, the test questions are different.

An answer key is provided for each multiple-choice test.

Coverage

The purpose of the chapter review quizzes is to assess whether students have acquired foundational knowledge of each chapter's content to enable them to apply the skill. Although the focus of each quiz is knowledge and comprehension of chapter content, quizzes may include application questions that provide hypothetical situations for evaluating students' ability to apply the skill.

Instructional Uses

Although the quizzes are intended as assessment tools, they can be used instructionally in several different ways:
1. Treat the quiz as an open-book exam, allowing students to locate the answers in the text. This activity will provide students with the opportunity to review chapter content and realize what skills are emphasized.
2. Ask students to predict or write questions they think will be on the quiz and then compare their predictions with the actual quiz. This activity will help students to determine what is important in each chapter, as well as to develop an important test-taking strategy.
3. Treat each quiz as a collaborative learning activity. Students can discuss each item and identify sections in the chapter that establish their choices as correct.
4. Use the quiz as a chapter preview. Allow students to skim or read the quiz questions before reading the chapter. The questions will establish an intent to remember chapter content.

PRACTICE TESTS

The practice tests are designed to measure students' ability to apply the skills learned in each chapter. Each test consists of a short excerpt from a college-level textbook followed by objective questions about vocabulary, comprehension, and the specific skills covered in that chapter. An answer key is provided for each test. The practice tests can be used as additional exercises or as competency-based tests for evaluative purposes.

PART ONE

CHAPTER QUIZZES

SET A

CHAPTER 1
Successful Attitudes Toward Reading and Learning

Directions: *Select the answer that best completes each statement.*

_____ 1. A common mistake that some beginning college students make is thinking that academic success depends upon

    (a) adjusting how they read and learn.

    (b) thinking critically about what they read.

    (c) increasing how much they study.

    (d) memorizing a large number of facts.

_____ 2. All of the following approaches will help you build a positive attitude toward college-level work *except*

    (a) accepting personal responsibility for your learning.

    (b) visualizing the problems you might encounter.

    (c) establishing long-term goals for yourself.

    (d) sending yourself positive messages.

_____ 3. To build your concentration you should

    (a) study in a different place every day.

    (b) control your environment.

    (c) focus on one subject for an entire evening.

    (d) work without breaks.

_____ 4. Learning style refers to

    (a) how well a person is able to learn.

    (b) how quickly a person learns.

    (c) the way a person learns.

    (d) how much a person remembers.

_____ 5. In contrast to a pragmatic learner, a creative learner feels more comfortable

    (a) working with others.

    (b) studying alone.

    (c) following rules.

    (d) taking risks.

_____ 6. A person with an auditory learning style would tend to learn more easily by

    (a) hearing.

    (b) reading.

    (c) studying pictures.

    (d) drawing diagrams.

_____ 7. As you read new material, one positive signal that you comprehend the material you are reading is that you

    (a) need to reread sentences and paragraphs often.

    (b) must use the author's language to explain an idea.

    (c) can see where the author is leading.

    (d) often slow down or lose your place.

_____ 8. The best way to try to understand a complicated idea is to

    (a) reread the previous paragraph.

    (b) skim the material for unfamiliar words.

    (c) take frequent breaks.

    (d) rephrase and explain each idea in your own words.

_____ 9. One strategy to improve your comprehension when you have little or no background knowledge about a topic is to

    (a) skim through the material before reading.

    (b) read the material aloud.

    (c) refer to other sources such as an encyclopedia or a more basic text.

    (d) skip introductory information.

_____ 10. If you are having difficulty following how reading material has been organized, it would be _least_ helpful to

    (a) pay more attention to headings.

    (b) read the summary.

    (c) write an outline based on the material.

    (d) read the material to a friend.

CHAPTER 2
Using Context Clues

Directions: *Using context clues, select the answer that most clearly states the meaning of the italicized word as it is used in the sentence.*

_____ 1. Both comedians were *seasoned* performers—each had appeared before an audience over 200 times.

    (a) challenging

    (b) experienced

    (c) aged

    (d) imposing

_____ 2. The dog was *submissive*—crouching, flattening its ears, and avoiding eye contact.

    (a) friendly and excitable

    (b) aggressive

    (c) yielding to the control of another

    (d) active

_____ 3. There was a *consensus*—or unified opinion—among the students that the exam was difficult.

    (a) requirement

    (b) consequence

    (c) disagreement

    (d) agreement

_____ 4. For their own safety, household pets should be *confined* to their own yard.

    (a) controlled

    (b) restricted

    (c) surrounded

    (d) determined

_____ 5. The quarterback *sustained* numerous injuries: a fractured wrist, two broken ribs, and a hip injury.

    (a) caused

    (b) experienced

    (c) displayed

    (d) noticed

_____ 6. The child remained *demure* while the teacher scolded, but became violently angry afterwards.

   (a) quiet and reserved

   (b) boisterous

   (c) cowardly

   (d) upset and distraught

_____ 7. Your *dossier* is a record of your credentials, including college transcripts and letters of recommendation.

   (a) briefcase or valise

   (b) statement of account

   (c) list

   (d) collection of papers

_____ 8. When preparing job application letters, develop one standard letter or *prototype*, then write variations of that letter to fit the specific jobs for which you are applying.

   (a) variation

   (b) model

   (c) detail

   (d) introduction

_____ 9. Although most members of the class agreed with the instructor's evaluation of the film, several strongly *objected*.

   (a) disagreed

   (b) obliterated

   (c) debated

   (d) consented

_____ 10. Sam's brother advised him to be *wary* of strangers he meets on the street.

   (a) suspicious

   (b) trusting

   (c) congenial with

   (d) generous toward

CHAPTER 3
Learning Word Parts

Directions: *Select the answer that provides the best definition for each word.*

_____ 1. multistage rocket

    (a) rocket with two stages

    (b) rocket with three stages

    (c) rocket with several stages

    (d) multipurpose rocket

_____ 2. nonpartisan

    (a) unwilling to reveal attitudes or feelings

    (b) unable to perform a task

    (c) not associated with a political party

    (d) unwilling to change

_____ 3. equilateral

    (a) having two sides

    (b) having uneven sides

    (c) not having sides

    (d) having all sides equal

_____ 4. triennial

    (a) happening every year

    (b) happening every two years

    (c) happening every three years

    (d) happening every four years

_____ 5. transcultural

    (a) differences in cultures

    (b) within cultures

    (c) among cultures

    (d) extending across cultures

_____ 6. chronometer

    (a) machine to control velocity

    (b) device to control friction

    (c) instrument for measuring time

    (d) instrument for measuring speed

_____ 7. disaffiliated

    (a) not associated

    (b) partially associated

    (c) several associations

    (d) false associations

_____ 8. territory

    (a) an area of land

    (b) related to fear

    (c) related to water

    (d) resulting from terror

_____ 9. astrology

    (a) study of stars

    (b) study of sound

    (c) a type of heat

    (d) a type of lens

_____ 10. photosensitive cell

    (a) cell sensitive to heat

    (b) cell sensitive to light

    (c) cell sensitive to color

    (d) cell sensitive to friction

CHAPTER 4
Learning New Words

Directions: *Select the answer that best completes each statement.*

_____ 1. The etymology of a word is its

    (a) pronunciation.

    (b) antonym.

    (c) history.

    (d) part of speech.

_____ 2. To find the meaning of an important word in the field of nursing, the best source to use would be

    (a) an unabridged dictionary.

    (b) a subject area dictionary.

    (c) a pocket or paperback dictionary.

    (d) a thesaurus.

_____ 3. A thesaurus is a dictionary of

    (a) antonyms.

    (b) pronunciation keys.

    (c) synonyms.

    (d) variations in spelling.

_____ 4. In addition to the definition of a word, a dictionary entry typically includes all of the following information about the word *except* its

    (a) part of speech.

    (b) origin.

    (c) restrictive meanings.

    (d) common misspellings.

_____ 5. To use the pronunciation key in the dictionary, you must know

    (a) which symbols correspond to which sounds.

    (b) how various sounds are grouped.

    (c) how to divide the words into syllables.

    (d) which abbreviations correspond to which words.

_____ 6. In a dictionary entry, meanings are arranged according to

    (a) alphabetical order.

    (b) the order in which they were developed.

    (c) part of speech.

    (d) level of difficulty.

_____ 7. Guide words in a dictionary are intended to help you

    (a) locate an entry rapidly.

    (b) read an entry more rapidly.

    (c) locate the right meaning quickly.

    (d) locate synonyms.

_____ 8. The word papaya would be found on the dictionary page with the guide words

    (a) palm / panicky.

    (b) panicle / par.

    (c) parish / part.

    (d) pass / pastiche.

_____ 9. The index card system for learning new words is effective because the system

    (a) is convenient to use during spare time.

    (b) incorporates context clues and word parts.

    (c) eliminates learning words in a fixed order.

    (d) does all of the above.

_____ 10. The number of syllables in the word circulation is

    (a) two.

    (b) three.

    (c) four.

    (d) five.

CHAPTER 5
Reading as Thinking

Directions: *Select the answer that best completes each statement.*

_____ 1. Previewing written material is a way of

    (a) familiarizing yourself with the material's content and organization.

    (b) testing your knowledge of the subject.

    (c) drawing inferences and conclusions from the material.

    (d) determining the author's patterns of thought.

_____ 2. When previewing a textbook chapter, you should read all of the following *except*

    (a) the last paragraph.

    (b) review questions.

    (c) the introductory paragraph.

    (d) references and footnotes.

_____ 3. Recalling background information helps a student to

    (a) preview more easily.

    (b) retain content and read more easily.

    (c) write summaries and outlines.

    (d) read faster.

_____ 4. Brainstorming is the process of

    (a) asking questions.

    (b) mentally outlining reading material.

    (c) recalling personal experiences.

    (d) writing down everything about a topic that comes to mind.

_____ 5. Developing guide questions is primarily intended to

    (a) give you practice answering test questions.

    (b) improve your retention and recall.

    (c) force you to read.

    (d) eliminate distractions.

_____ 6. The easiest way to form guide questions is to use the

  (a) introduction.

  (b) review questions.

  (c) summary.

  (d) headings.

_____ 7. Of the following questions, the best one to ask for a section in your history text on the Revolutionary War would be

  (a) When did it start?

  (b) Where did it start?

  (c) Why did it start?

  (d) How long did it last?

_____ 8. All of the following are useful to do before reading a chapter *except*

  (a) skimming the chapter for its organization.

  (b) reading the glossary.

  (c) reading the headings.

  (d) thinking about what you already know about the topic.

_____ 9. The "S" step of SQ3R involves

  (a) processing.

  (b) previewing.

  (c) brainstorming.

  (d) reviewing.

_____ 10. Of the following activities, the one that should be part of the "recite" step of SQ3R is

  (a) brainstorming to activate your background knowledge.

  (b) answering guide questions formed when you previewed.

  (c) looking over the organization of the material.

  (d) rereading chapter titles and headings.

CHAPTER 6
Understanding Sentences

_____ 1. An example of a coordinate sentence that combines two equally important ideas is

  (a) They thought Jack was a sore loser, but he really was just upset with himself.

  (b) Although Pete felt tired, he went to the party.

  (c) Of course, I expected to receive a passing grade.

  (d) After Pete left the party, he walked home.

_____ 2. An example of a subordinate sentence that expresses one key idea and a related idea is

  (a) She wanted to stay; I wanted to leave.

  (b) The stock is selling at a price below its book value.

  (c) I left the party early, but my sister decided to stay.

  (d) While I was waiting for the bus, I finished my math assignment.

Directions: *Use the following sentence to answer questions 3–6.*

Trees under attack by insects release a chemical into the air.

_____ 3. The key idea of this sentence is that

  (a) trees are attacked.

  (b) trees release a chemical.

  (c) chemicals are in the air.

  (d) insects attack trees.

_____ 4. The subject of the sentence is

  (a) trees.

  (b) insects.

  (c) chemicals.

  (d) air.

_____ 5. The phrase "under attack by insects" describes

  (a) the trees.

  (b) how trees protect themselves.

  (c) the chemicals.

  (d) the air.

_____ 6. The phrase "into the air"

    (a) describes the chemical.

    (b) refers to trees.

    (c) tells where chemicals are released.

    (d) refers to insects.

Directions: _Select the answer that is the best paraphrase of each of the following sentences._

_____ 7. Because of the power of emotions and feelings and the effects they can have, they can be used destructively in numerous ways: to control, to damage, to manipulate, or to create guilt.

    (a) Feelings and emotions have powerful effects and can be harmful; they can control, injure, shape, or create guilt.

    (b) Emotions can be used destructively in many ways.

    (c) The power of emotions and feelings is destructive.

    (d) Guilt and injury often result if feelings and emotions become too powerful.

_____ 8. We often get advice from "authorities," people assumed to be knowledgeable because of their experience or position, and seldom question their advice.

    (a) Authorities are people who have many accomplishments and who give advice.

    (b) We get advice from and seldom challenge authorities, people who are experts due to their accomplishments or positions.

    (c) We respect authorities due to their accomplishments or position.

    (d) Authorities are accomplished people who give advice.

_____ 9. For most people in a society such as the United States, the most important life goal is to have a successful and dignified occupation or career that provides an adequate income and a comfortable lifestyle.

    (a) A common life goal in the United States is to have a successful career that provides income to support a comfortable way of life.

    (b) To be worthwhile, a career or occupation must provide dignity and respect.

    (c) Careers must be dignified and produce income.

    (d) A comfortable lifestyle is the most important life goal for most people in the United States.

_____ 10. Most political scientists are still uncertain about the effect of television on our values; however, its effect on our opinions is clearly established.

    (a) Political scientists know that television has a clear effect on our opinions and values.

    (b) According to political scientists, television has no effect on values but does influence opinion.

    (c) Political scientists are unsure how television affects us.

    (d) According to political scientists, television affects our opinions and may also affect our values.

CHAPTER 7
Understanding Paragraphs: Topics, Stated Main Ideas, and Implied Main Ideas

Directions: *Select the answer that best completes each statement.*

_____ 1. The topic of a paragraph is the

    (a) subject of the paragraph.

    (b) main point of the paragraph.

    (c) noun that is the subject of a sentence.

    (d) object of the predicate.

_____ 2. Most of the sentences in a paragraph

    (a) restate the main idea.

    (b) explain the main idea.

    (c) provide examples.

    (d) do not connect to each other.

_____ 3. The best clue to use in identifying the topic of a paragraph is

    (a) the arrangement of the sentences.

    (b) the use of directional words.

    (c) a frequently repeated key word.

    (d) the order of details.

_____ 4. Of the following groups of words, the one that contains one general term and three specific terms is

    (a) Time, Golf Digest, Newsweek, U.S. News and World Report.

    (b) students, classmates, colleagues, friends.

    (c) vanilla, raspberry, chocolate, strawberry.

    (d) newspapers, media, radio, television.

_____ 5. Of the following groups of words, the one that contains one general term and three specific terms is

    (a) North America, South America, Africa, Australia.

    (b) snow, rain, sleet, hail.

    (c) rap, blues, rock, country.

    (d) broccoli, corn, vegetables, squash.

_____ 6. In a paragraph, the topic sentence usually is the

    (a) first sentence.

    (b) second sentence.

    (c) middle sentence.

    (d) last sentence.

_____ 7. A writer would place a topic sentence at the beginning and end of a paragraph in order to

    (a) lead up to the main idea and then explain it.

    (b) lead the reader to a conclusion.

    (c) emphasize an important idea.

    (d) express an opinion.

_____ 8. If a paragraph does not have a stated topic sentence, then the

    (a) paragraph does not have a main idea.

    (b) paragraph lacks organization and focus.

    (c) reader must infer its main idea.

    (d) details are more important.

Directions: _For each of the following statements, select the choice that best explains what the writer is implying but has not directly stated._

_____ 9. The sociology exam was a breeze.

    (a) The exam had too many questions.

    (b) The exam was about the effects of wind.

    (c) The exam was easy.

    (d) The exam room was windy.

_____ 10. Carole was supposed to reserve a meeting room last month but she dropped the ball.

    (a) Carole forgot to reserve the meeting room.

    (b) Carole reserved the meeting room a week ago.

    (c) Carole was playing ball instead of making the reservations.

    (d) Carole couldn't find a meeting room to reserve.

CHAPTER 8
Understanding Paragraphs: Supporting Details and Transitions

Directions: *Select the answer that best completes each statement.*

_____ 1. In a paragraph, the details that directly explain the main idea are called

    (a) major details.

    (b) minor details.

    (c) key details.

    (d) implied details.

_____ 2. A writer uses examples primarily to

    (a) prove that an idea is correct.

    (b) make an idea real and understandable.

    (c) lead the reader back to the main idea.

    (d) tell why a main idea is correct.

_____ 3. In order to explain how to do something, a writer would most likely use supporting details such as

    (a) reasons.

    (b) facts.

    (c) steps and procedures.

    (d) statistics.

_____ 4. The primary function of transitional words in a paragraph is to

    (a) provide facts and statistics.

    (b) signal a writer's direction of thought.

    (c) indicate the location of the main idea.

    (d) provide a list of key details.

_____ 5. Terms such as "on the other hand," "however," and "in contrast" indicate a

    (a) continuation of thought.

    (b) change in thought.

    (c) cause-effect relationship.

    (d) list will follow.

_____ 6. The transitional phrase below that indicates a comparison is

    (a) "in addition."

    (b) "next."

    (c) "similarly."

    (d) "further."

_____ 7. Paraphrasing a paragraph involves all of the following _except_

    (a) rewording using synonyms.

    (b) rearranging the order of ideas.

    (c) including your opinions and reactions.

    (d) maintaining the author's focus and emphasis.

_____ 8. One guideline for paraphrasing paragraphs is to

    (a) work sentence-by-sentence.

    (b) not worry about the author's focus or emphasis.

    (c) add your own ideas about the material.

    (d) only include one important idea in each paragraph.

_____ 9. The type of transition that presents ideas in the order in which they happened is called

    (a) continuation.

    (b) enumeration.

    (c) summation.

    (d) time-sequence.

_____ 10. The type of transition that indicates that the writer will draw his or her ideas together is called

    (a) summation.

    (b) example.

    (c) cause-effect.

    (d) contrast.

CHAPTER 9
Following the Author's Thought Patterns

Directions: *Select the answer that best completes each statement.*

_____ 1. It is useful to learn thought patterns because they

    (a) identify the author's purpose.

    (b) improve your vocabulary.

    (c) improve your comprehension.

    (d) function as a transition.

_____ 2. A paragraph that explains a technique for analyzing a poem by discussing and analyzing excerpts from several poems uses the

    (a) cause/effect pattern.

    (b) illustration/example pattern.

    (c) definition pattern.

    (d) comparison/contrast pattern.

_____ 3. The two parts of a definition are its

    (a) general group or class and its distinguishing characteristics.

    (b) associative features and its distribution characteristics.

    (c) associative features and its distinguishing characteristics.

    (d) general group or class and its associative features.

_____ 4. The thought pattern that is most concerned with relationships between events is

    (a) classification.

    (b) cause/effect.

    (c) definition.

    (d) illustration/example.

_____ 5. To write a paragraph describing how to load a disk into a computer, you would most likely use the

    (a) cause/effect pattern.

    (b) comparison/contrast pattern.

    (c) chronological order/process pattern.

    (d) illustration/example pattern.

_____ 6. Of the following topics, the one that would most likely be developed using the cause/effect pattern is

    (a) the treatment of mental disorders.

    (b) how to take objective exams.

    (c) preparing your income tax form.

    (d) limitations of context clues.

_____ 7. If you wrote a paragraph explaining that there are two types of exams—objective and essay—the pattern you should use is

    (a) chronological order/process.

    (b) classification.

    (c) cause/effect.

    (d) definition.

_____ 8. One characteristic of the cause/effect pattern is that it

    (a) is always concerned with single causes and single effects.

    (b) focuses on similarities among events.

    (c) may express multiple causes and multiple effects.

    (d) focuses on visualization skills.

_____ 9. One characteristic of a paragraph that discusses both similarities and differences is that it

    (a) can be organized only one way.

    (b) can use one of several means of organization.

    (c) usually discusses similarities and then differences.

    (d) must be concerned with only one type of difference.

_____ 10. Of the following topics, the one that would most likely be developed using the chronological order/process pattern is

    (a) the psychology of humor.

    (b) a comparison of personality theories.

    (c) stages of child development.

    (d) types of intimacy.

CHAPTER 10
Reading Textbook Chapters

Directions: *Select the answer that best completes each statement.*

_____ 1. Information about the audience for whom a text is written is often included in the

    (a) appendix.

    (b) table of contents.

    (c) first chapter.

    (d) preface.

_____ 2. All of the following are considered typographical aids *except*

    (a) headings and subheadings.

    (b) colored print.

    (c) italic print.

    (d) photographs.

_____ 3. The primary purpose of graphic aids is to

    (a) organize and simplify information.

    (b) provide sources for further study.

    (c) make a text appear more complicated.

    (d) divide the text into separate parts.

_____ 4. When studying an illustration, each of the following would be helpful activities *except*

    (a) going back and forth between the text and the illustration.

    (b) reading the title of the illustration to find out what it is intended to show.

    (c) writing an outline of the text.

    (d) testing your understanding of the illustration by drawing and labeling one of your own.

_____ 5. The glossary provides

    (a) an outline of the text.

    (b) discussion and/or review questions.

    (c) a mini-dictionary of important vocabulary used in the text.

    (d) a list of important dates mentioned in the text.

_____ 6. As compared to other types of textbooks, technical writing typically

    (a) contains fewer graphs and charts.

    (b) is more factually dense.

    (c) uses fewer specialized words.

    (d) lacks general and specific terms.

_____ 7. The _least_ helpful strategy for learning vocabulary in an anatomy and physiology course would be to

    (a) learn key prefixes, roots, and suffixes.

    (b) learn to pronounce each new term.

    (c) make use of the glossary.

    (d) skip over difficult terminology.

_____ 8. In the first chapter of a textbook, you would be most likely to find

    (a) diagrams and graphs.

    (b) references and authorities consulted.

    (c) important terminology.

    (d) typographical aids.

_____ 9. A preface typically includes all of the following _except_

    (a) the author's major points of emphasis.

    (b) a review of key terms used in the text.

    (c) a description of learning aids contained in the text.

    (d) information on how the text is organized.

_____ 10. The learning aid that would be most useful in preparing for an essay exam is

    (a) italicized words and phrases.

    (b) review questions.

    (c) vocabulary lists.

    (d) discussion questions.

CHAPTER 11
Reading Graphic and Electronic Information

Directions: *Select the answer that best completes each statement.*

_____ 1. The subject of a graphic is typically identified in its

(a) key.

(b) scale.

(c) title.

(d) legend.

_____ 2. A diagram is commonly used to

(a) express a relationship between two or more items.

(b) show causes or effects.

(c) demonstrate relationships between parts of an object.

(d) compare events over time.

_____ 3. The graphic that would best demonstrate the frequency of child abuse among various parental age groups is

(a) a flowchart.

(b) a diagram.

(c) an organizational chart.

(d) a bar graph.

_____ 4. In a sociology course Anne traced her family history. The chart that would best depict her findings is

(a) an organizational chart.

(b) a linear graph.

(c) a pictogram.

(d) a pie chart.

_____ 5. If you were to create a chart showing the gradual increase in your heating bills over the last ten years, the best type of chart to use would be

(a) an organizational chart.

(b) a linear graph.

(c) a pictogram.

(d) a pie chart.

6. Ivan wants to create a graphic comparing changes in yearly earnings of Hispanic and African-American workers over the past ten years in the following age groups: under 20, 20–40, and 40–60. The graphic that would best depict his findings is a

    (a) diagram.

    (b) multiple bar graph.

    (c) flowchart.

    (d) pie chart.

7. A flowchart is often used to

    (a) describe distance and location.

    (b) organize large amounts of statistical data.

    (c) show how something is organized.

    (d) explain a process.

8. A CD-ROM should *not* be used

    (a) as a chapter preview.

    (b) in place of your textbook.

    (c) for review and practice.

    (d) to help you study for exams.

9. A location on the Internet where people can correspond about a particular topic or issue is known as a

    (a) newsgroup.

    (b) web site.

    (c) home page.

    (d) header.

10. Web sites are useful information sources when researching a topic because they

    (a) are all sponsored by educational institutions.

    (b) often include links to other information.

    (c) have already been verified as reliable sources.

    (d) always include the credentials of the person who created the site.

CHAPTER 12
Organizing and Remembering Information

Directions: *Select the answer that best completes each statement.*

_____ 1. The most effective way to highlight is to

(a) read a paragraph first and then highlight what is important.

(b) highlight entire sentences.

(c) highlight only the topic sentence in each paragraph.

(d) highlight as you read.

_____ 2. As a general rule, the amount of your reading material that you should highlight is

(a) less than 5 percent.

(b) 20–30 percent.

(c) 50 percent.

(d) 75 percent.

_____ 3. In deciding what to highlight, the most helpful part of a textbook would be

(a) chapter introductions.

(b) graphic aids.

(c) headings.

(d) summaries.

_____ 4. In a textbook, all of the following are items that might be appropriate to mark as well as highlight *except*

(a) definitions.

(b) possible test questions.

(c) confusing passages.

(d) chapter titles.

_____ 5. Outlining material is a good way to

(a) have a dialogue with the writer.

(b) record the writer's organization.

(c) make inferences about what you have read.

(d) avoid studying from the textbook.

_____ 6. Of the following situations, summarizing would be most effective for

    (a) reading the newspaper.

    (b) describing the plot of a film or short story for a literature course.

    (c) preparing for a multiple choice exam.

    (d) showing the organization of a biology lecture.

_____ 7. Immediate review is done

    (a) right after you have finished reading an assignment.

    (b) periodically throughout the semester.

    (c) as needed when studying for exams.

    (d) before you begin reading an assignment.

_____ 8. During periodic review, you should

    (a) reread the entire text.

    (b) highlight key ideas.

    (c) prepare outlines.

    (d) review your highlighting or notetaking.

_____ 9. The most effective method to use when reading library reference books to complete a term paper would be

    (a) highlighting and marking.

    (b) outlining.

    (c) periodic review.

    (d) immediate review.

_____ 10. In writing a summary it is always important to

    (a) include your opinion of the subject matter.

    (b) write a topic sentence.

    (c) include examples and as many supporting details as possible.

    (d) use the author's words as much as possible.

CHAPTER 13
Interpreting the Writer's Message and Purpose

Directions: *Select the answer that best completes each statement.*

_____ 1. Of the following words, the one that usually carries a strong connotative meaning is

    (a) pencil.

    (b) reasoning.

    (c) building.

    (d) sex.

_____ 2. An inference is

    (a) an expression of fact.

    (b) a broad, general statement.

    (c) something that is assumed to be true.

    (d) a prediction about the unknown based on available facts and information.

_____ 3. Of the following statements, the one that is a figurative expression is

    (a) Walking in the rain is fun.

    (b) My dream dried up like a raisin.

    (c) Ideas are often subject to critical evaluation.

    (d) I wandered down the deserted street.

_____ 4. Suppose you were given a $1,000 bill by a stranger. An inference that you might make about the situation is that

    (a) the stranger is wealthy.

    (b) you are his friend.

    (c) you are a student.

    (d) the stranger was wearing a black hat.

_____ 5. A figurative expression is often

    (a) literal.

    (b) factual.

    (c) an example.

    (d) a comparison.

_____ 6. Of the following situations, the one in which an inference was made is

   (a) A student in your class leaves the room in the middle of an exam.

   (b) Your instructor wears the same blue suit every day.

   (c) The sky is darkening and you think it may rain soon.

   (d) You finished your exam in psychology before everyone else so you left the room.

_____ 7. A writer's tone can best be described as the writer's

   (a) feeling about the subject.

   (b) purpose for writing.

   (c) style.

   (d) objective content.

_____ 8. A magazine article titled "World Terrorism: A Demand for New Get-Tough Policy" is most likely intended to

   (a) explain.

   (b) persuade.

   (c) amuse.

   (d) entertain.

_____ 9. Of the following statements, the one that uses subjective language is

   (a) Body language is a form of communication.

   (b) Men are hounded unmercifully by women.

   (c) Fast food is low in nutritional value.

   (d) Nuclear war may be caused by human error.

_____ 10. Of the following statements, the one that uses descriptive language is

   (a) Names beginning with J are currently popular.

   (b) Women resent domination by men.

   (c) A kiss is intended to bring good luck.

   (d) The restaurant serves bland, colorless, thinly disguised TV-dinner style food.

CHAPTER 14
Evaluating: Asking Critical Questions

Directions: *Select the answer that best completes each statement.*

_____ 1. Knowing the source of an article is important in evaluating its

    (a) accuracy and value.

    (b) style.

    (c) assumptions.

    (d) generalizations.

_____ 2. An assumption is an idea that the writer

    (a) proves.

    (b) disagrees with.

    (c) approaches logically.

    (d) believes to be true.

_____ 3. Of the following articles, the one that is most likely to be slanted is

    (a) "How to Take Better Photographs."

    (b) "Repairing Foreign-Make Cars."

    (c) "Careers in the Health Sciences."

    (d) "Leisure Time Is Wasted Time."

_____ 4. A generalization is a

    (a) broad statement about a group based on experience with some members of that group.

    (b) statement of fact that is subsequently proven.

    (c) form of logical progression.

    (d) statement of right or wrong.

_____ 5. Of the following statements, the one that expresses a generalization is

    (a) I learned more than I ever expected in that course.

    (b) This course was my favorite.

    (c) All instructors at the college are highly committed to helping students.

    (d) Dr. Vilardo is a chemistry professor.

_____ 6. Of the following statements, the one that expresses a value judgment is

    (a) The engineer accepted a bribe.

    (b) Accepting a bribe is against the law.

    (c) This country values prestige more than defense.

    (d) I expect the restaurant to be expensive.

_____ 7. In reading and evaluating a writer's value judgment, it is important to

    (a) always begin by disagreeing with the writer.

    (b) notice whether the writer makes generalizations.

    (c) take a position, either agreeing or disagreeing.

    (d) determine whether the writer offers evidence to support the value judgment.

_____ 8. The use of statistics as evidence is

    (a) always acceptable proof.

    (b) sometimes misleading.

    (c) never acceptable proof.

    (d) only acceptable in technical writing.

_____ 9. Writing is considered slanted it if

    (a) is based entirely on opinion.

    (b) is objective and factual.

    (c) presents only a negative point of view.

    (d) involves the selection and omission of information.

_____ 10. When evaluating an Internet source, it would *not* be helpful to

    (a) look for the sponsoring organization of the site.

    (b) determine the purpose of the posting.

    (c) analyze the author's use of figurative language.

    (d) cross-check the information against other sources.

ANSWER KEY
Chapter Quizzes
Set A

Chapter 1

1.	d	2.	b	3.	b	4.	c	5.	d
6.	a	7.	c	8.	d	9.	c	10.	d

Chapter 2

1.	b	2.	c	3.	d	4.	b	5.	b
6.	a	7.	d	8.	b	9.	a	10.	a

Chapter 3

1.	c	2.	c	3.	d	4.	c	5.	d
6.	c	7.	a	8.	a	9.	a	10.	b

Chapter 4

1.	c	2.	b	3.	c	4.	d	5.	a
6.	c	7.	a	8.	b	9.	d	10.	c

Chapter 5

1.	a	2.	d	3.	b	4.	d	5.	b
6.	d	7.	c	8.	b	9.	b	10.	b

Chapter 6

1.	a	2.	d	3.	b	4.	a	5.	a
6.	c	7.	a	8.	b	9.	a	10.	d

Chapter 7

1.	a	2.	b	3.	c	4.	d	5.	d
6.	a	7.	c	8.	c	9.	c	10.	a

Chapter 8

| 1. | c | 2. | b | 3. | c | 4. | b | 5. | b |
| 6. | c | 7. | c | 8. | a | 9. | d | 10. | a |

Chapter 9

| 1. | c | 2. | b | 3. | a | 4. | b | 5. | c |
| 6. | a | 7. | b | 8. | c | 9. | b | 10. | c |

Chapter 10

| 1. | d | 2. | d | 3. | a | 4. | c | 5. | c |
| 6. | b | 7. | d | 8. | c | 9. | b | 10. | d |

Chapter 11

| 1. | c | 2. | c | 3. | d | 4. | a | 5. | b |
| 6. | b | 7. | d | 8. | b | 9. | a | 10. | b |

Chapter 12

| 1. | a | 2. | b | 3. | c | 4. | d | 5. | b |
| 6. | b | 7. | a | 8. | d | 9. | b | 10. | b |

Chapter 13

| 1. | d | 2. | d | 3. | b | 4. | a | 5. | d |
| 6. | c | 7. | a | 8. | b | 9. | b | 10. | d |

Chapter 14

| 1. | a | 2. | d | 3. | d | 4. | a | 5. | c |
| 6. | c | 7. | d | 8. | b | 9. | d | 10. | c |

CHAPTER QUIZZES

SET B

CHAPTER 1
Successful Attitudes Toward Reading and Learning

Directions: *Select the answer that best completes each statement.*

_____ 1. For every hour you spend in class, you should study outside of class for

(a) one half hour.

(b) one hour.

(c) two hours.

(d) three hours.

_____ 2. To help overcome poor concentration, you should

(a) read in a place where you feel very comfortable.

(b) choose a time of day when you are most relaxed.

(c) study at different times during the day.

(d) read in the same place every day.

_____ 3. One way to focus your attention is to

(a) spend an entire evening on one subject.

(b) avoid taking breaks until you have completed all of your work.

(c) set goals and time limits for yourself.

(d) reward yourself before you begin studying.

_____ 4. One positive comprehension signal is

(a) making connections among ideas.

(b) rereading sentences or paragraphs frequently.

(c) struggling to stay with the author.

(d) slowing down or losing your place.

_____ 5. The best learning strategy for an applied learner would be to

(a) talk aloud when studying.

(b) think of practical situations related to the topic.

(c) focus on organizational patterns.

(d) try to visualize events.

_____ 6. Visual learners tend to learn more easily by

    (a) listening.

    (b) seeing.

    (c) experimenting.

    (d) speaking.

Directions: _Match the learning problem described in the left-hand column with the most appropriate strategy in the right-hand column._

Learning Problem

Strategy

_____ 7. Difficult or unfamiliar words

a. Rephrase or explain each idea in your own words

_____ 8. Poorly organized material

b. Obtain background information from other sources

_____ 9. Unfamiliar topic

c. Use context and analyze word parts

_____ 10. Complicated or difficult ideas

d. Write an outline

CHAPTER 2
Using Context Clues

Directions: *Using context clues, select the answer that most clearly states the meaning of the italicized word as it is used in the sentence.*

_____ 1. The lawyer tried to confuse the jury by bringing in many facts that weren't *pertinent* to the case.

  (a) obvious

  (b) continuous

  (c) relevant

  (d) harmful

_____ 2. There were many things about the library that made it *conducive* to study, including good lighting and many reference books.

  (a) unattractive

  (b) cold

  (c) helpful

  (d) sociable

_____ 3. Little Jill hid shyly behind her mother when she met new people, yet her brother Matthew was very *gregarious.*

  (a) insulting

  (b) sociable

  (c) concerned

  (d) embarrassed

_____ 4. The elderly man was often *fractious* with strangers, but with his family he was good-natured and easy to get along with.

  (a) generous

  (b) trustworthy

  (c) grouchy

  (d) agreeable

_____ 5. To qualify for high-security jobs, applicants must undergo a *battery* of tests designed to measure physical and mental aptitude.

(a) series

(b) single

(c) connection

(d) question

_____ 6. When several members of the president's staff were charged with various crimes, the public's confidence in the government *eroded*.

(a) grew

(b) deteriorated

(c) healed

(d) repeated

_____ 7. The noise in the nursery school was *incessant*; the crying, yelling, and laughing never stopped.

(a) careless

(b) harmful

(c) bold

(d) continuous

_____ 8. Dogs, cats, parakeets, and other *sociable* pets can provide senior citizens with companionship.

(a) weak

(b) friendly

(c) dangerous

(d) unattractive

_____ 9. Freshmen are often *naive* about college at first, but by their second semester they are usually quite sophisticated in the ways of their new school.

(a) innocent

(b) experienced

(c) annoyed

(d) concerned

_____ 10. People who suffer from migraine headaches are frequently advised to avoid things that can *precipitate* an attack, such as chocolate and some cheeses.

(a) prevent

(b) trigger

(c) follow

(d) delay

CHAPTER 3
Word Parts

Directions: *Select the proper word part for the space in each sentence.*

_____ 1. Fortunately, the window was still _____broken after it suddenly slammed shut.

    (a) se

    (b) trans

    (c) un

    (d) vis

_____ 2. Can you en_____ion what you will be doing five years from now?

    (a) voc

    (b) vis

    (c) im

    (d) en

_____ 3. Since Tim conquered his acro_____, he no longer is afraid to climb ladders.

    (a) photo

    (b) ology

    (c) phobia

    (d) gamy

_____ 4. The photographs provided _____ification that Christy had indeed won the race.

    (a) uni

    (b) im

    (c) ver

    (d) homo

_____ 5. It was difficult to find Rick because all the men were wearing _____forms.

    (a) mono

    (b) uni

    (c) gram

    (d) un

_____ 6. The _____ain was obviously too rocky for either farming or grazing.

    (a) tele

    (b) terr

    (c) micro

    (d) geo

_____ 7. The minister's in_____ation began in the chapel service.

    (a) vid

    (b) bi

    (c) poly

    (d) voc

_____ 8. I decided to _____plant the bush to a different location.

    (a) mis

    (b) trans

    (c) terr

    (d) im

_____ 9. _____odynamics is concerned with the relationships between heat and the mechanical energy of work.

    (a) therm

    (b) theo

    (c) hetero

    (d) pseudo

_____ 10. In _____spect, I wish I had studied harder for the exam.

    (a) in

    (b) retro

    (c) ex

    (d) intro

CHAPTER 4
Learning New Words

Directions: *Select the answer that best completes each statement.*

_____ 1. Guide words can help you

    (a) pronounce a word in the dictionary.

    (b) find a word in the dictionary.

    (c) define a word in the dictionary.

    (d) identify word parts.

_____ 2. In a dictionary, restrictive meanings refer to words that are

    (a) not accepted as standard English.

    (b) no longer in common usage.

    (c) used in a specific field of study.

    (d) borrowed from another language.

_____ 3. A thesaurus lists

    (a) word origins.

    (b) definitions.

    (c) synonyms.

    (d) parts of speech.

_____ 4. You might use a thesaurus in all of the following situations *except* to

    (a) locate a word that fits a particular situation.

    (b) replace a word that is unclear.

    (c) locate a word that is more descriptive.

    (d) check the specialized or technical meaning of a word.

_____ 5. The syllable of a word that is stressed most heavily is the one by the

    (a) hyphen.

    (b) bold accent mark.

    (c) abbreviation.

    (d) pronunciation key.

_____ 6. The history of a word is called its

    (a) synonym.

    (b) antonym.

    (c) idiom.

    (d) etymology.

_____ 7. When you look up the meaning of a new word in the dictionary, you must choose the meaning that fits the way the word is used in the

    (a) definition.

    (b) sentence context.

    (c) thesaurus.

    (d) pronunciation key.

_____ 8. The number of syllables in the word <u>magnificent</u> is

    (a) two.

    (b) three.

    (c) four.

    (d) five.

_____ 9. The word <u>eminent</u> would be found on the dictionary page with the guide words

    (a) elsewhere / embryo.

    (b) embryology / employment.

    (c) emporium / encumber.

    (d) eject / electrocute.

_____ 10. In dictionary entries, the parts of speech are shown by letters in

    (a) boldfaced print.

    (b) abbreviations.

    (c) guide words.

    (d) italics.

CHAPTER 5
Reading as Thinking

Directions: *Select the answer that best completes each statement.*

_____ 1. Previewing reading material is a way to

    (a) highlight important information in each paragraph.

    (b) familiarize yourself with facts and details.

    (c) get an overview of the material.

    (d) develop conclusions.

_____ 2. The first paragraph in each chapter usually provides

    (a) review questions.

    (b) an overview of the section.

    (c) patterns of thought.

    (d) an outline.

_____ 3. Boldfaced headings are important because they usually

    (a) identify the topic of the material.

    (b) provide background information about the author.

    (c) present summaries of the material.

    (d) reveal the author's bias.

_____ 4. Typographical aids are

    (a) introductions to reading material.

    (b) features that help to organize and highlight information.

    (c) end-of-chapter discussion questions.

    (d) summaries and outlines.

_____ 5. The SQ3R system helps a student to

    (a) preview more easily.

    (b) mentally outline reading material.

    (c) comprehend and remember reading material.

    (d) read faster.

_____ 6. The "S" step of SQ3R involves

    (a) brainstorming.

    (b) reviewing.

    (c) previewing.

    (d) processing.

_____ 7. The "3R" steps of SQ3R refer to

    (a) read, research, and reread.

    (b) read, review, and reread.

    (c) read, recite, and review.

    (d) review, recite, and research.

_____ 8. End-of-chapter material usually includes

    (a) vocabulary lists and discussion questions.

    (b) graphs and charts.

    (c) marginal notes.

    (d) typographical aids.

_____ 9. Graphs, charts and pictures included in textbook chapters will usually

    (a) help you to outline the material.

    (b) provide you with discussion questions.

    (c) point you toward the most important information.

    (d) suggest sources for further research.

_____ 10. Guide questions should be asked

    (a) before previewing.

    (b) after previewing but before reading.

    (c) after reading.

    (d) during review.

CHAPTER 6
Understanding Sentences

Directions: *Select the answer that is the best paraphrase of each of the following sentences.*

_____ 1. One way to lower fat in your diet is to eliminate meat with marbling. Also, eat more low-fat dairy products such as skim milk and read labels carefully to see how much fat is part of a certain food.

    (a) Lower fat in your diet by eliminating meats with marbling.

    (b) Look for fat-free products to reduce fat in your diet.

    (c) You can lower the amount of fat in your diet by selecting meat without marbling, eating low-fat dairy products, and reading labels carefully.

    (d) Read ingredients on food labels to find the fat content of the product.

_____ 2. One way to fight stress is to exercise regularly, since exercise releases physical tension. Other good methods include using relaxation techniques, as well as talking to friends, a member of the clergy, or a therapist.

    (a) Exercise is a good way to fight stress.

    (b) Talking to a therapist can reduce stress.

    (c) You can fight stress by exercising regularly, using relaxation methods, and talking with others.

    (d) Talking to friends, clergymen, or a therapist can help reduce stress.

_____ 3. Owning a pet can make a person feel less lonely, reduce blood pressure, and encourage exercise.

    (a) Owning a pet can encourage a person to exercise more.

    (b) Owning a pet has a number of advantages.

    (c) A pet can help a person feel less lonely in life.

    (d) A pet can help reduce a person's blood pressure.

_____ 4. Children with dyslexia often have difficulty distinguishing between different shapes and identifying letters, and they may fail to develop a preference for using the right or left hand.

    (a) Children with dyslexia have difficulty identifying letters.

    (b) There are several signs that a child has dyslexia.

    (c) A dyslexic child may not develop a preference for using his or her right or left hand.

    (d) An inability to distinguish different shapes can be a sign of dyslexia.

_____ 5. Some cases of permanent baldness are caused by heredity, while temporary baldness is the result of certain types of drugs or high fevers.

   (a) Baldness may be attributed to heredity, drugs, or illness.

   (b) Temporary baldness is the result of drugs or illness.

   (c) Permanent baldness is caused by heredity.

   (d) Baldness can be temporary or permanent.

_____ 6. Vitamin C has been proven to help prevent illness, reduce the severity of colds, and help people enhance the capabilities of their immune systems.

   (a) Vitamin C can help prevent colds.

   (b) People can increase the abilities of their immune systems by taking vitamin C.

   (c) Vitamin C has many beneficial uses.

   (d) The severity of colds and illnesses can be decreased by taking vitamin C.

_____ 7. Smoking has been banned on commercial airline flights and in many restaurants as a result of new legislation. Magazines and television producers have also joined in the campaign against smoking.

   (a) Smoking is not permitted in many restaurants.

   (b) New laws prohibit smoking on commercial airline flights.

   (c) Smoking is no longer as acceptable in our society as it once was.

   (d) Magazines and television producers have joined the campaign against smoking.

Directions: _Use this sentence to answer questions 8–10:_ The king ruled his country with an iron hand.

_____ 8. The key idea of this sentence is that the king is

   (a) friendly.

   (b) evil.

   (c) strict.

   (d) unable to lead.

_____ 9. The subject of the sentence is

   (a) the country.

   (b) an iron hand.

   (c) the king.

   (d) rules.

_____ 10. The phrase "iron hand" means

   (a) made of metal.

   (b) strict and forceful.

   (c) friendly.

   (d) uncertain.

CHAPTER 7
Understanding Paragraphs: Topics, Stated Main Ideas, and Implied Main Ideas

Directions: *Select the answer that best completes each statement.*

_____ 1. The four essential parts of a paragraph are

    (a) details, examples, transitions, and ideas.

    (b) the topic, the main idea, details, and transitions.

    (c) the stated main idea, the implied main idea, the topic, and examples.

    (d) transitions, examples, questions, and facts.

_____ 2. The main idea of a paragraph is usually expressed in the

    (a) transitional phrases.

    (b) first example.

    (c) topic sentence.

    (d) specific details.

_____ 3. To find the topic of a paragraph, you should ask yourself

    (a) What is the one thing the author is discussing throughout the paragraph?

    (b) What kinds of examples does the author use?

    (c) How does the author seem to feel about the material?

    (d) What is the author's background?

_____ 4. To imply an idea means to

    (a) reason out an idea based on what has been stated.

    (b) suggest an idea but not state it directly.

    (c) create connections between ideas.

    (d) provide support for an idea.

_____ 5. In order to find an implied main idea, it would be *least* helpful to

    (a) find the topic of the paragraph.

    (b) decide what the writer wants you to know about the topic.

    (c) express the idea in your own words.

    (d) determine how the paragraph is developed.

Directions: *For each set of specific ideas below, select the general idea that best describes it.*

_____ 6. Specific ideas: dogs, canaries, tigers, elephants, panda bears

    (a) household pets

    (b) animals

    (c) endangered animals

    (d) zoo animals

_____ 7. Specific ideas: alcohol, tobacco, heroin

    (a) liquids

    (b) illegal substances

    (c) addictive substances

    (d) legal substances

_____ 8. Specific ideas: for better health, to fit into old clothes, for vanity

    (a) reasons to visit your doctor

    (b) reasons to go on a diet

    (c) reasons to take vitamins

    (d) reasons to buy new clothes

_____ 9. Specific ideas: mosquito, wasp, gnat, butterfly

    (a) living creatures

    (b) pests

    (c) insects

    (d) harmful insects

_____ 10. Specific ideas: Martha Washington, Hillary Clinton, Jacqueline Kennedy

    (a) famous twentieth century women

    (b) famous American parents

    (c) wives of American presidents

    (d) famous wives

CHAPTER 8
Understanding Paragraphs: Supporting Details and Transitions

Directions: *Select the answer that best completes each statement.*

_____ 1. Minor details typically are *not* used to

(a) provide additional information.

(b) offer examples.

(c) further explain one of the key details.

(d) directly support or prove the main idea.

_____ 2. Linking words or phrases used to lead the reader from one idea to another are called

(a) key details.

(b) supporting details.

(c) major details.

(d) transitions.

_____ 3. In order to provide evidence that the main idea is correct, a writer often uses

(a) examples.

(b) procedures.

(c) facts and statistics.

(d) descriptions.

_____ 4. The transition words "because" and "consequently" indicate that the writer is showing

(a) a cause-effect relationship between two or more things or events.

(b) each idea in order of importance.

(c) how the previous idea is different from what follows.

(d) how the previous idea is similar to what follows.

Directions: *Read the paragraph below and then answer the questions that follow on the next page.*

1. Several types of experiences influence how people feel about being touched. 2. Our experiences as a child are one thing that affects our attitudes towards touching. 3. Little girls, for example, are generally kissed and hugged more than little boys. 4. As a result, women often like touching more than men. 5. Our feelings about being touched also depend on our cultural background. 6. Latin Americans and southern Europeans, for example, casually touch each other more than northern Europeans and most Americans. 7. Social context, as well, influences our willingness to touch and be touched. 8. Even men who are usually uneasy about touching may hug one another at an exciting sporting event.

_____ 5. A good heading for an outline of this paragraph would be

    (a) Types of Childhood Experiences.

    (b) Types of Experiences That Influence How Men and Women Feel About Being Touched.

    (c) Why Some People Like Being Touched.

    (d) How Men and Woman Feel About Each Other.

_____ 6. The key details of the paragraph are

    (a) Latin Americans, southern Europeans, and men at sporting events.

    (b) childhood experiences, cultural background, and social context.

    (c) willingness to be touched, and discomfort at being touched.

    (d) little girls, little boys, and differences in being touched.

_____ 7. The first key detail is signaled by the transitional word(s)

    (a) one.

    (b) for example.

    (c) also.

    (d) as well.

_____ 8. Sentence 5 provides

    (a) a minor detail.

    (b) a key detail.

    (c) the topic sentence.

    (d) the main idea.

_____ 9. Sentence 6 provides

    (a) a minor detail.

    (b) a key detail.

    (c) the topic sentence.

    (d) the main idea.

_____ 10. The best paraphrase of sentence 8 is

    (a) Most men are uncomfortable about touching.

    (b) Men who are usually uncomfortable about touching may hug at an exciting sports event.

    (c) Most men are unwilling to touch and be touched unless they're participating in a sport.

    (d) Men who are uneasy about touching usually enjoy sporting events.

CHAPTER 9
Following the Author's Thought Patterns

Directions: *For each of the following items, select the answer that identifies the writer's thought pattern.*

_____ 1. To borrow money, consumers can choose among several sources: banks, finance companies, and insurance companies.

    (a) chronological order/process

    (b) classification

    (c) comparison/contrast

    (d) cause/effect

_____ 2. Transitions are words and phrases that show relationships between ideas. For instance, time transitions such as *before*, *soon*, and *now* show time relationships.

    (a) classification

    (b) comparison/contrast

    (c) cause/effect

    (d) illustration/example

_____ 3. Experts who study employment trends expect an increased demand for certain types of jobs, including accountants, teachers, chefs, and nurses.

    (a) definition

    (b) classification

    (c) comparison/contrast

    (d) chronological order/process

_____ 4. Eleanor Roosevelt received threatening letters after her husband became president. Therefore, the secret service insisted she carry a pistol.

    (a) chronological order/process

    (b) classification

    (c) comparison/contrast

    (d) cause/effect

_____ 5. High school friendships are often different from newer friendships. Old friends can share memories, but new friends are more likely to share current interests.

    (a) classification

    (b) definition

    (c) comparison/contrast

    (d) cause/effect

_____ 6. Cut the box along the dotted lines. Then, remove the plastic bag and empty the cake mix into a bowl.

    (a) chronological order/process

    (b) classification

    (c) comparison/contrast

    (d) cause/effect

_____ 7. Like butter, most margarine is 99 percent fat and contains about one hundred calories per tablespoon. Margarine, however, contains less saturated fat than butter.

    (a) illustration/example

    (b) cause/effect

    (c) comparison/contrast

    (d) definition

_____ 8. One method psychologists use is observation. Observation involves watching others and recording what occurs. For instance, child psychologists often observe children through one-way mirrors.

    (a) chronological order/process

    (b) classification

    (c) cause/effect

    (d) illustration/example

_____ 9. Tim decided to save time by washing his dark clothes with his white ones. As a result, his white dress shirts are now an ugly grayish pink.

    (a) classification

    (b) comparison/contrast

    (c) definition

    (d) cause/effect

_____ 10. Students who are most likely to drop out of school share a number of family characteristics.

    (a) chronological order/process

    (b) classification

    (c) comparison/contrast

    (d) definition

CHAPTER 10
Reading Textbook Chapters

Directions: *Select the answer that best completes each statement.*

_____ 1. In a textbook, the preface is where you would find

      (a) a list of vocabulary words.

      (b) charts and graphs.

      (c) the author's introduction to the text.

      (d) a list of the book's chapters.

_____ 2. A glossary and index usually are located

      (a) at the front of the text.

      (b) at the end of the text.

      (c) in the preface of the text.

      (d) within each textbook chapter.

_____ 3. The table of contents is

      (a) a list of vocabulary words.

      (b) a typographical aid.

      (c) a list of references.

      (d) an outline of the text.

_____ 4. Typographical aids include

      (a) italic type.

      (b) maps.

      (c) photographs.

      (d) charts.

_____ 5. In a textbook, important vocabulary words are listed and defined in the

      (a) appendix.

      (b) table of contents.

      (c) glossary.

      (d) preface.

_____ 6. When reading technical material, you should plan to do all of the following *except*

(a) read the material more slowly and carefully than other textbooks.

(b) record important information in your own words.

(c) reread and review various sections several times.

(d) highlight all facts and details.

_____ 7. Information on how a text is organized can be found in its

(a) index.

(b) opening chapter.

(c) preface.

(d) glossary.

_____ 8. The first thing to read when studying an illustration is its

(a) abbreviations or symbols.

(b) title or caption.

(c) scale.

(d) source.

_____ 9. Enumeration refers to the

(a) practical introductory information that follows the preface.

(b) learning aids included in the index.

(c) numbering or lettering of facts and ideas within a paragraph.

(d) subheadings listed in the table of contents.

_____ 10. In contrast to the review questions at the end of a chapter, discussion questions typically

(a) cover factual content only.

(b) are more helpful in preparing for an objective exam.

(c) deal with interpretations or applications of the material.

(d) ask students to list, describe, or explain.

CHAPTER 11
Reading Graphic and Electronic Information

Directions: *Select the answer that best completes each statement.*

_____ 1. A pie chart is used to illustrate

    (a) how a process or procedure works.

    (b) causes and effects.

    (c) how parts of a unit have been divided or classified.

    (d) a comparison of events over time.

_____ 2. The best graphic to illustrate weight increases in girls between the ages of two and eighteen would be

    (a) a pie chart.

    (b) a line graph.

    (c) an organizational chart.

    (d) a flowchart.

_____ 3. Flowcharts help a reader to

    (a) compare events over time.

    (b) show causes and effects.

    (c) visualize each step or stage in a process.

    (d) express relationships between items.

_____ 4. The best graphic for illustrating the death toll resulting from addictive drugs in the United States would be a

    (a) flowchart.

    (b) line graph.

    (c) pictogram.

    (d) bar graph.

_____ 5. When studying a graphic, it is *most* important to recognize the

    (a) type of data used.

    (b) units of change.

    (c) source of the data.

    (d) general trend or pattern.

_____ 6. If your psychology instructor asked you to create a chart illustrating the stages of memory loss, the type of chart you should use is a

(a) pictogram.

. (b) flowchart.

(c) linear graph.

(d) bar graph.

_____ 7. The type of graph shown to the right is called

(a) a line graph.

(b) a bar graph.

(c) a flowchart.

(d) an organizational chart.

_____ 8. A Web site is a

(a) newspaper section.

(b) home page.

(c) location on the Internet.

(d) chat room.

_____ 9. All of the following statements about Web sites are true *except*

(a) Only qualified professionals can place Web sites on the Internet.

(b) Web sites usually provide links to other sites that offer related information.

(c) Web sites often have the most current information.

(d) The Web site's address indicates its source as educational, governmental, commercial, or other.

_____ 10. If you wanted to list facts and figures in a series of columns or rows, the graphic you would use is a

(a) table.

(b) linear graph.

(c) diagram.

(d) flowchart.

CHAPTER 12
Organizing and Remembering Information

Directions: *Select the answer that best completes each statement.*

_____ 1. When highlighting material you should start by

    (a) reading a paragraph or section.

    (b) summarizing the material.

    (c) creating an outline.

    (d) paraphrasing ideas.

_____ 2. Highlighting and marking important facts as you read are effective methods of

    (a) making predictions about the reading.

    (b) identifying and organizing information.

    (c) mapping the material.

    (d) reading faster.

_____ 3. As a general rule, you should highlight no more than

    (a) 10 percent of the material.

    (b) 20 to 30 percent of the material.

    (c) 40 to 50 percent of the material.

    (d) 50 to 75 percent of the material.

_____ 4. An effective way to react to an author's ideas in a chapter is to

    (a) summarize the chapter.

    (b) create an outline.

    (c) make notes in the margin.

    (d) create a map.

_____ 5. Outlining helps you to do all of the following *except*

    (a) record information from reference books you do not own.

    (b) develop new ways of organizing the writer's ideas.

    (c) test your understanding of what you read.

    (d) understand how ideas are related.

_____ 6. When creating an outline, it is most important to

  (a) include everything that is included in the original passage.

  (b) make sure you use capital and lowercase letters.

  (c) be sure that all of the information underneath a heading supports that heading.

  (d) include exact wording from the text, as well as all facts and details.

_____ 7. Mapping involves

  (a) summarizing information in a chapter.

  (b) creating an outline from the chapter.

  (c) drawing diagrams to how ideas in a chapter are related.

  (d) numbering ideas in order of importance.

_____ 8. If you wanted to write a brief statement about a chapter, the technique that would be most useful is

  (a) marking.

  (b) highlighting.

  (c) mapping.

  (d) summarizing.

_____ 9. As compared to an outline, a summary typically is

  (a) less objective.

  (b) longer.

  (c) more opinionated.

  (d) less detailed.

_____ 10. Periodic review involves

  (a) going back over information from time to time.

  (b) creating an outline.

  (c) immediately reviewing work you have just completed.

  (d) writing a summary of your work.

CHAPTER 13
Interpreting the Writer's Message and Purpose

Directions: *Select the answer that best completes each statement.*

_____ 1. A word's connotative meaning is its

    (a) exact dictionary meaning.

    (b) synonym.

    (c) implied meaning.

    (d) literal meaning.

_____ 2. A reasoned or educated guess is called

    (a) a fact.

    (b) an inference.

    (c) an opinion.

    (d) a denotation.

_____ 3. When a writer uses language that makes sense on an imaginative level but not on a factual level, the writer is using

    (a) figurative language.

    (b) connotative language.

    (c) denotative language.

    (d) literal language.

_____ 4. The purpose of descriptive language is to

    (a) persuade the reader to take action.

    (b) present facts objectively.

    (c) help the reader visualize the subject.

    (d) give the author's opinion about a subject.

_____ 5. Objective language is language that

    (a) expresses attitudes and feelings.

    (b) is factual.

    (c) expresses an author's tone.

    (d) is persuasive.

_____ 6. The sentence that is an example of subjective language is

   (a) Cable television has brought many changes to the industry.

   (b) Children are exposed to more than a thousand hours of television before they enter kindergarten.

   (c) Greedy television producers and sponsors must start taking responsibility for the programs they broadcast.

   (d) There are many reasons why our society is so changing.

Directions: _Select the answer that identifies the tone of the following statements._

_____ 7. The best thing to do when you feel the urge to exercise is to lie down until the feeling goes away.

   (a) instructive

   (b) persuasive

   (c) humorous

   (d) nostalgic

_____ 8. Put the book back on the shelf when you are through reading it.

   (a) instructive

   (b) persuasive

   (c) humorous

   (d) nostalgic

_____ 9. I can remember when our house was surrounded by trees and furry little animals. Now when I look outside my window all I see is a highway.

   (a) instructive

   (b) persuasive

   (c) humorous

   (d) nostalgic

_____ 10. We need to start caring more about the rights of baby seals. They are defenseless against the people who kill them for their pelts.

   (a) instructive

   (b) persuasive

   (c) humorous

   (d) nostalgic

CHAPTER 14
Evaluating: Asking Critical Questions

Directions: *Select the answer that best completes the statement.*

_____ 1. When evaluating an article's accuracy, it is important to verify its

    (a) tone.

    (b) style.

    (c) inferences.

    (d) source.

_____ 2. An idea, theory, or principle that a writer believes to be true is called

    (a) an assumption.

    (b) a fact.

    (c) a bias.

    (d) a generalization.

_____ 3. A writer who presents a one-sided view of a subject is said to be

    (a) critical.

    (b) objective.

    (c) biased.

    (d) factual.

_____ 4. Slanted writing refers to the presentation of

    (a) all the facts.

    (b) all the details.

    (c) statistics.

    (d) only those details that suit the author's purpose.

_____ 5. A generalization is a statement made about a group of people based on

    (a) experience with some members of that group.

    (b) a variety of published sources.

    (c) facts.

    (d) statistics.

_____ 6. The statement that is a statistic is

    (a) In Seattle it rains six months out of the year.

    (b) Planets in our solar system rotate around the sun.

    (c) People who own pets are usually responsible and sensitive to the needs of their pets.

    (d) Television is the cause of all violence in schools around the country.

_____ 7. The statement that is a generalization is

    (a) The drinking age in the United States is twenty-one.

    (b) Several incidents of violence have occurred over the past few years.

    (c) Smoking is a major cause of lung cancer.

    (d) Pit bulls are vicious, dangerous dogs.

_____ 8. The statement that is a fact is

    (a) The voting age in America is eighteen.

    (b) Evergreen trees are the best for creating privacy around your back yard.

    (c) Couples should date for at least two years before getting married.

    (d) Dogs make the best pets.

_____ 9. The statement that is an opinion is

    (a) Zinc has been proven to be an effective way to fight colds.

    (b) Dieting can slow down a person's metabolism.

    (c) Manhattan is the best place to see a play or musical.

    (d) A Maltese dog is one breed of dog that doesn't shed.

_____ 10. The statement that is a value judgment is

    (a) Married couples who have children should not get divorced.

    (b) Test scores in schools have decreased over the years.

    (c) Many elderly people can benefit by owning a pet.

    (d) Violence in the news may desensitize people to violence in real life situations.

ANSWER KEY
Chapter Quizzes
Set B

Chapter 1

1.	c	2.	d	3.	c	4.	a	5.	b
6.	b	7.	c	8.	d	9.	b	10.	a

Chapter 2

1.	c	2.	c	3.	b	4.	c	5.	a
6.	b	7.	d	8.	b	9.	a	10.	b

Chapter 3

1.	c	2.	b	3.	c	4.	c	5.	b
6.	b	7.	d	8.	b	9.	a	10.	b

Chapter 4

1.	b	2.	c	3.	c	4.	d	5.	b
6.	d	7.	b	8.	c	9.	b	10.	d

Chapter 5

1.	c	2.	b	3.	a	4.	b	5.	c
6.	c	7.	a	8.	a	9.	c	10.	b

Chapter 6

1.	c	2.	c	3.	b	4.	b	5.	a
6.	c	7.	c	8.	c	9.	c	10.	b

Chapter 7

1.	b	2.	c	3.	a	4.	b	5.	d
6.	b	7.	c	8.	b	9.	c	10.	c

Chapter 8

| 1. | d | 2. | d | 3. | c | 4. | a | 5. | b |
| 6. | b | 7. | a | 8. | b | 9. | a | 10. | b |

Chapter 9

| 1. | b | 2. | d | 3. | b | 4. | d | 5. | c |
| 6. | a | 7. | c | 8. | d | 9. | d | 10. | b |

Chapter 10

| 1. | c | 2. | b | 3. | d | 4. | a | 5. | c |
| 6. | d | 7. | c | 8. | b | 9. | c | 10. | c |

Chapter 11

| 1. | c | 2. | b | 3. | c | 4. | d | 5. | d |
| 6. | b | 7. | b | 8. | c | 9. | a | 10. | a |

Chapter 12

| 1. | a | 2. | b | 3. | b | 4. | c | 5. | b |
| 6. | c | 7. | c | 8. | d | 9. | d | 10. | a |

Chapter 13

| 1. | c | 2. | b | 3. | a | 4. | c | 5. | b |
| 6. | c | 7. | c | 8. | a | 9. | d | 10. | b |

Chapter 14

| 1. | d | 2. | a | 3. | c | 4. | d | 5. | a |
| 6. | a | 7. | d | 8. | a | 9. | c | 10. | a |

PART TWO

PRACTICE TESTS

SET A

CHAPTER 1
Successful Attitudes Toward Reading and Learning

Directions: *Read the selection, then answer the questions that follow.*

Coin-operated vending machines are a tried-and-true way to sell convenience goods, especially cigarettes and drinks. These machines are appealing because they require minimal space and personnel to maintain and operate.

Some of the most interesting innovations are state-of-the-art vending machines, which dispense everything from Ore-Ida french fries to software. French consumers can even purchase Levi's jeans from a machine called Libre Service which offers the pants in 10 different sizes. The Japanese are also avid users of vending machines. These machines, a cluster of which can be found on many street corners, dispense virtually all of life's necessities, plus many luxuries people in other countries would not consider obtaining from a machine. The list includes jewelry, fresh flowers, frozen beef, business cards, and even underwear.

In general, vending machines are best suited to the sales of inexpensive merchandise and food and beverages. Most consumers are reluctant to buy pricey items from a machine. New vending machines may spur more interest, however, with technological developments such as video kiosk machines that let people see the product in use, the ability to accept credit cards as payment, and inventory systems that signal the operator when malfunctions or stock-outs occur.

--adapted from *Marketing: Real People, Real Choices*, p. 429

_____ 1. The main point of this selection is that

   (a) vending machines offer inexpensive items only.

   (b) vending machines are popular in France and Japan.

   (c) a variety of products are available through vending machines.

   (d) new vending machines can accept credit cards as payment.

_____ 2. According to the selection, vending machines are an appealing way to sell convenience goods because they

   (a) do not require a large investment of money.

   (b) require minimal space and personnel to maintain and operate.

   (c) generate a great deal of profits from high-dollar items.

   (d) allow the owners to set their own prices for items.

_____ 3. The purpose of Libre Service is to

    (a) dispense food and beverages only.

    (b) show people different products in use.

    (c) signal the operator when malfunctions or stock-outs occur.

    (d) sell Levi's jeans in ten different sizes.

_____ 4. The description of Japanese people as "avid users of vending machines" means that they

    (a) are enthusiastic about using vending machines for purchases.

    (b) prefer not to buy food products from machines.

    (c) only buy certain hard-to-find luxury items from vending machines.

    (d) have difficulty finding vending machines in Japan.

_____ 5. While reading this passage, one signal that would suggest that you are *not* comprehending it would be

    (a) you can predict what will come next.

    (b) everything in the passage seems to fit and make sense.

    (c) you read at a regular, comfortable pace.

    (d) you must use the author's language to explain an idea.

CHAPTER 2
Using Context Clues

Directions: *Read the following selection, then use context to determine the meaning of the underlined words from the selection.*

As Europeans began to travel to the Americas and the West Indies, they returned with many native foods from those regions such as chocolate, chilies, beans, corn, tomatoes, and potatoes. Some of these items were <u>initially</u> avoided and treated with suspicion since they looked different and were often regarded as poisonous. Through the efforts of pioneers such as French agronomist Antoine-August Parmentier and American scientist George Washington Carver, deep-seated fears and misconceptions about different foods were <u>dispelled</u>. Parmentier successfully began a campaign in 1774 that made potatoes a <u>staple</u> on the French dinner table. Research efforts led by Carver resulted in over 300 products including cheese, milk, flour, and coffee made from peanuts.

Once people began <u>emigrating</u> from Europe to the "New Worlds" of North America, they brought along their favorite drinks, breads, desserts, herbs, spices, and fruits. These old favorites were combined with new foods, creating <u>distinctive</u> regional cuisines from New England clam chowder to hominy grits.

--adapted from *Tourism: The Business of Travel*, p. 127

_____ 1. initially

    (a) continuously

    (b) permanently

    (c) at first

    (d) painfully

_____ 2. dispelled

    (a) spread

    (b) eliminated

    (c) agreed

    (d) gathered

_____ 3. staple

    (a) metal fastener

    (b) type of fruit

    (c) unpopular ingredient

    (d) essential food

_____ 4. emigrating

     (a) moving

     (b) shopping

     (c) refusing

     (d) allowing

_____ 5. distinctive

     (a) distasteful

     (b) special

     (c) disastrous

     (d) complicated

CHAPTER 3
Using Word Parts

Directions: *Read the following selection, then use word parts to determine the meaning of the underlined words from the selection.*

Passenger rail service had its origins in Europe in 1825. Four years later, North America welcomed the advent of passenger rail service when the South Carolina and Canal Railroad began carrying passengers between South Carolina and Georgia with steam-powered locomotives. Transcontinental service in the United States began in 1869 and in Canada in 1885.

Long-distance rail travel was given a boost in the United States when George Pullman developed the Pullman coach, with sleeping facilities for overnight travel. The addition of dining cars, and food and lodging facilities pioneered by Fred Harvey, introduced the golden age of passenger railroad service in the United States. Dissatisfied with poor food and service, Harvey arranged in 1875 to provide food service for the Atchison, Topeka, and Santa Fe Railroad at its Topeka depot; eventually, the railroad awarded him all of its dining car services.

Passenger rail service flourished and was an important form of domestic transportation in Canada and the United States until the 1940s.

--adapted from *Tourism: The Business of Travel*, p. 81

_____ 1. advent

   (a) arrival

   (b) territory

   (c) study

   (d) removal

_____ 2. transcontinental

   (a) underground

   (b) across the continent

   (c) around an area

   (d) not connected

_____ 3. introduced

   (a) led to

   (b) did not allow

   (c) left behind

   (d) sent away

_____ 4. dissatisfied

     (a) agreed

     (b) promoted

     (c) overly pleased

     (d) not content

_____ 5. transportation

     (a) concerned with feelings

     (b) related to land

     (c) method of carrying something

     (d) term of measurement

CHAPTER 4
Learning New Words

Directions: *Read the selection, then use a dictionary to answer the following questions about the underlined words.*

Alexander Hamilton at 34 had already proved himself a remarkable man. Born in the British West Indies, the illegitimate son of a <u>shiftless</u> Scot who was little better than a beachcomber, and raised by his mother's family, he came to New York in 1773 to attend King's College. When the Revolution broke out, he joined the army. At 22 he was a staff <u>colonel</u>, aide-de-camp to Washington. Later, at Yorktown, he led a line regiment, displaying a bravery approaching <u>foolhardiness</u>. He married the daughter of Philip Schuyler, a wealthy and influential New Yorker, and after the Revolution he practiced law in that state.

Hamilton was a bundle of <u>contradictions</u>. Witty, charming, possessed of a mind like a sharp knife, he was sometimes the soul of practicality, sometimes an incurable romantic. No more hard-headed realist ever lived, yet he was quick to resent any slight to his honor, even—tragically—ready to fight a duel though he <u>abhorred</u> the custom of dueling.

--adapted from *The American Nation,* p. 153

_____ 1. The definition of "shiftless" is

    (a) dangerous.

    (b) restless.

    (c) able to accomplish what is needed.

    (d) lacking ambition or purpose.

_____ 2. The best representation of the way to pronounce "colonel" is

    (a) call uh null.

    (b) col uh null.

    (c) co lo nee ull.

    (d) cur null.

_____ 3. As a part of speech, the word "foolhardiness" is

    (a) a verb.

    (b) a noun.

    (c) an adjective.

    (d) an adverb.

_____ 4. The syllable that is most heavily stressed in "contradictions" is

    (a) con.

    (b) tra.

    (c) dic.

    (d) tions.

_____ 5. The best synonym for the word "abhorred" is

    (a) hated.

    (b) respected.

    (c) admired.

    (d) practiced.

Name: _____ Date: _____ Section: _____

CHAPTER 5
Reading as Thinking

Directions: *Read the selection, then answer the questions that follow.*

Although most of us recognize that listening is an important skill, many of us have trouble tuning in to things we don't relate to. What does it take to be an excellent listener? According to experts, the better than average listener uses the following techniques and stays in the PRESENT!

- **Partnership:** The best listeners don't just sit back and receive information; they participate as partners. Eye contact is a good start, but it's not enough. As listeners, we must be engaged in the process—nodding, asking questions, and using body language are all important in the partnership of listening.

- **Reviewing Systematically:** If your mind starts to wander, get focused. Paraphrase what you hear, ask for clarity in meaning, restate key points, and summarize what you think are key points of interest.

- **Effort:** Try to take the initiative and be a proactive listener. Develop skills to cope with distraction and to compensate for speakers' shortfalls. Work on appropriate responses, including voice tone, gestures, and posture.

- **Star Events:** Sometimes a speaker's behavior—a word, phrase, facial mannerism, or style of speaking—can turn us off. Star events can stop our concentration and cause us to tune out the message. When star events bother you, force yourself to ask a question or restate the last words spoken.

- **Empathy:** Rather than always trying to respond with an intellectual tidbit, try focusing on the emotional aspects of spoken experiences.

- **Neutralize snap judgments:** Try to keep an open mind and squelch any tendency to judge others quickly.

- **Tenacity:** Excellent listeners participate in conversation by pursuing meanings and offering their thoughts. Remember to use all aspects of the PRESENT acronym rather than just being tenacious and your value as a listener will be increased.

   --adapted from *Access to Health*, p. 116

_____ 1. The main point of this selection is that
   (a) most people are poor listeners.
   (b) good listeners use several techniques.
   (c) boring speakers cause listeners to tune out.
   (d) it's important not to make snap judgments about speakers.

_____ 2. This selection uses all of the following typographical aids *except*

   (a) italics.

   (b) boldfaced type.

   (c) underlining.

   (d) enumeration (listing).

_____ 3. The most useful guide question for the heading "Partnership" would be

   (a) What is a partnership?

   (b) Who should form a partnership?

   (c) Does a partnership improve a person's listening skills?

   (d) How do listeners form a partnership with speakers?

_____ 4. The word "compensate" (under the heading "Effort") means to

   (a) make up for.

   (b) pay back.

   (c) pretend.

   (d) complain.

_____ 5. The "star events" described in the selection refer to

   (a) meetings that feature a celebrity as the main speaker.

   (b) aspects of a speaker's behavior that distract us from the message.

   (c) our pre-formed opinions about a speaker's ability.

   (d) the key points of interest in a speech.

CHAPTER 6
Understanding Sentences

Directions: *Read the selection, then answer the questions that follow.*

Climates in major urban areas usually differ markedly from those of surrounding rural landscapes. Typically cities are warmer, both in winter and in summer. Several factors contribute to these differences. First, cities lack large expanses of vegetation and soil that absorb rainfall and later allow it to evaporate. Evaporation cools the land surface, and without this evaporation the surface remains warmer. Second, the walls of buildings form vertical surfaces that help to trap solar energy during the daytime. Concrete, asphalt, and similar building materials store this heat and at night these warm surfaces shield the ground between buildings from exposure to a large expanse of relatively cool sky and thus keep it warmer than it would otherwise be. Third, air pollutants may absorb heat and keep the air warmer. Finally, heat released from energy use, such as in heating buildings, adds to the heat available in the city (although this amount is very small in comparison to the amount of energy derived from the sun).

--adapted from *Introduction to Geography*, p. 83

_____ 1. The purpose of this selection is to
   (a) explain why climates in cities are different from rural areas.
   (b) describe the effects of pollution on urban areas.
   (c) compare the climates of cities throughout the world.
   (d) criticize developers for contributing to the warmer climates in cities.

_____ 2. The best paraphrase of the first sentence is
   (a) Climates in major urban areas are different.
   (b) Major urban areas are usually very different from the surrounding rural areas.
   (c) City climates are typically very different from nearby rural areas.
   (d) The climates of landscapes surrounding major urban areas are markedly different from the climates of other areas.

_____ 3. The subject of the second sentence is
   (a) cities.
   (b) are warmer.
   (c) winter.
   (d) summer.

_____ 4. Air pollutants contribute to the warmer climate in cities by

   (a) preventing evaporation.

   (b) absorbing heat.

   (c) shielding the ground between buildings.

   (d) generating solar energy.

_____ 5. The best synonym for the word "derived" (in the last sentence) is

   (a) obtained.

   (b) absorbed.

   (c) hidden.

   (d) misused.

CHAPTER 7
Understanding Paragraphs: Topics, Stated Main Ideas, and Implied Main Ideas

Directions: *Read the selection, then answer the questions that follow.*

The federal government has a handful of **government corporations**. These are not exactly like private corporations in which you can buy stock and collect dividends, but they *are* like private corporations—and different from other parts of the government—in two ways. First, they provide a service that *could be* handled by the private sector. Second, they typically charge for their services, though often at rates cheaper than those the consumer would pay to a private-sector producer.

The granddaddy of the government corporations is the Tennessee Valley Authority (TVA). Established in 1933 as part of the New Deal, it has controlled floods, improved navigation, protected the soil against erosion, and provided inexpensive electricity to millions of Americans in Tennessee, Kentucky, Alabama, and neighboring states. Through Comsat—a modern-day government corporation that sells time-sharing on NASA satellites—you can rent time on a space satellite for radio communications. The Post Office, one of the original cabinet departments (first headed by Benjamin Franklin) has become the government's largest corporation: the U.S. Postal Service.

--adapted from *Government in America*, p. 501

_____ 1. The purpose of this selection is to

    (a) describe government corporations.

    (b) compare private corporations to government corporations.

    (c) explain how private corporations are regulated by the government.

    (d) describe the origin of the U.S. Postal Service.

_____ 2. The topic sentence in the first paragraph is the

    (a) first sentence.

    (b) second sentence.

    (c) third sentence.

    (d) last sentence.

_____ 3. The topic of the second paragraph is

    (a) the Tennessee Valley Authority (TVA).

    (b) Comsat.

    (c) the U.S. Postal Service.

    (d) government corporations.

_____ 4. The word "sector" (in the third sentence) means

    (a) secret.

    (b) part or division.

    (c) leader.

    (d) choice.

_____ 5. According to the selection, the government's *oldest* corporation is

    (a) TVA.

    (b) Comsat.

    (c) the U.S. Postal Service.

    (d) NASA.

CHAPTER 8
Understanding Paragraphs: Supporting Details and Transitions

Directions: *Read the selection, then answer the questions that follow.*

Terri Morrison and Wayne Conaway are two Pennsylvania-based entrepreneurs who have succeeded by guiding executives through the white water rapids of international business etiquette. Their company, Getting Through Customs, was established in 1990 to help corporate clients understand and adapt to cultural differences.

The owners train executives to do business abroad by schooling them in local customs. On the company Web site, a traveler is told what he or she needs to know when conducting business overseas, such as local customs, conversation styles, and negotiating tactics. For example, their report on Colombia includes this kind of guidance: "Take the time to greet everyone formally. Men shake hands with each other and with women. Women choose whether or not to shake hands with other women; sometimes women will clasp each other's forearms instead. Friends are expected to hug and exchange kisses on the cheeks. When men hug each other, they often add a backslap or two."

The Web site also provides a selection of gifts with information regarding which are appropriate in different cultures. For instance, the firm includes this warning with its offer of a leather wallet: "As a product made of cowhide, it is inappropriate for persons who object to the use of leather. Do not give this, or any other cowhide product, to Hindus. Most Muslims object to pig leather but not necessarily to cowhide. If you give this wallet to a devout Muslim, be sure to mention what kind of leather is used. Finally, some vegetarians and animal-rights supporters object to the use of leather. This is especially prevalent in the United Kingdom." This is the kind of advice that marketers need to navigate abroad—and avoid sinking in treacherous cultural waters.

--adapted from *Marketing: Real People, Real Choices*, p. 99

_____ 1. The purpose of this selection is to

    (a) explain why countries have different customs.

    (b) describe gifts that are appropriate in different countries.

    (c) illustrate how marketers use gifts to sell their products.

    (d) describe a company that helps clients understand cultural differences.

_____ 2. The main type of supporting details used in the second paragraph are

    (a) procedures.

    (b) examples.

    (c) reasons.

    (d) statistics.

_____ 3. In the third paragraph, the transitional word or phrase that indicates that an example will follow is

    (a) also.

    (b) For instance.

    (c) but.

    (d) Finally.

_____ 4. According to the selection, in Columbia it is customary for

    (a) men to shake hands with both men and women.

    (b) men to shake hands only with other men.

    (c) women to slap each other on the back when they meet.

    (d) men and women to give each other expensive gifts when they meet.

_____ 5. The word "prevalent" (in the last paragraph) means

    (a) promotion.

    (b) ideal.

    (c) common.

    (d) bad.

CHAPTER 9
Following the Author's Thought Patterns

Directions: *Read the selection, then answer the questions that follow.*

In 1273 the imperial crown of Germany was given to Count Rudolf (1273-1291) of the House of Habsburg, a name derived from Habichtsburg ("Castle of the Hawk"), the family's home in northern Switzerland. During the remainder of the Middle Ages, the Habsburgs had amazing success in territorial acquisition; Rudolf himself acquired Austria through marriage, and thereafter the Habsburgs ruled their holdings from Vienna.

In 1356 the German nobility won a significant victory in their efforts to avoid the creation of a powerful monarchy. The Golden Bull, a document that served as the political constitution of Germany until early in the nineteenth century, established a procedure by which seven German electors—three archbishops and four princes—chose the emperor. The electors and other important princes were given rights that made them virtually independent rulers, and the emperor could take no important action without the consent of the imperial feudal assembly, the Diet, which met infrequently.

From 1438 until 1806, the Habsburgs held the imperial crown almost without interruption. Maximilian I (1493-1519) helped make the Habsburgs the most important royal family in sixteenth-century Europe by marrying Mary of Burgundy, heiress of the rich Low Countries, and by marrying his son to the heiress of Spain.

Inspired by the accomplishments of other European monarchs, Maximilian attempted to strengthen the monarchy. His program for a national court system, army, and taxation was frustrated by the German princes who insisted on guarding "German freedom." The emperor continued to be limited in power and the empire was unsuccessful in establishing an imperial treasury, an efficient central administration, or a standing army.

> --adapted from *Civilization Past & Present*, pp. 237-238

_____ 1. The main thought pattern used throughout the selection is

   (a) definition.

   (b) comparison/contrast.

   (c) cause/effect.

   (d) chronological order.

_____ 2. Of the following phrases from the selection, the one that suggests the overall thought pattern of this selection is

(a) In 1273.

(b) which met infrequently.

(c) Inspired by the accomplishments.

(d) The emperor continued.

_____ 3. The main idea of the second paragraph is that

(a) the German nobility wanted to keep the monarchy from becoming powerful.

(b) three archbishops and four princes were responsible for choosing the emperor.

(c) the emperor gave the electors and other princes certain rights.

(d) the imperial feudal assembly did not meet very often.

_____ 4. The word "frustrated" (in the last paragraph) means

(a) angry.

(b) impatient.

(c) prevented.

(d) promoted.

_____ 5. The purpose of the last paragraph is to

(a) make comparisons among rulers.

(b) explain why Maximilian's efforts failed.

(c) define imperialism.

(d) describe the German princes.

CHAPTER 10
Reading Textbook Chapters

Directions: *Read the selection, then answer the questions that follow.*

The introduction is perhaps the most important single part of the speech, so be especially careful to avoid the most common faults.

1. **Don't Apologize.** Apologies generally are to be avoided. In much of the United States and Western Europe, an apology is seen as an excuse for a lack of competence or effectiveness. To apologize in your speech is to encourage your audience to look for faults and to alert them that your speech could have and should have been better. In many other cultures (for example, Japanese), however, the speaker is expected to begin with an apology. It's a way of complimenting the audience and placing them in a superior position. The speaker who doesn't apologize may be seen as arrogant and as one who feels superior to the audience.

2. **Don't Make Hollow Promises.** Don't promise something that you will not in fact deliver. The speaker who promises to tell you how to improve your love life, or how to make a fortune in the stock market, or how to be the most popular person on campus, and fails to deliver such insight, quickly loses credibility.

3. **Don't Rely on Gimmicks.** Avoid gimmicks that gain attention but are irrelevant to the nature of the speech or are inconsistent with your treatment of the topic. Thus, for example, slamming a book on the desk or telling a joke that bears no relation to the rest of your speech may accomplish this very limited goal of gaining attention. The audience, however, quickly sees them for what they are—gimmicks and tricks that have fooled them into paying attention. Such actions are resented and will set up barriers between you and your listeners.

—adapted from *The Elements of Public Speaking*, pp. 273-274

_____ 1. The purpose of this selection is to

   (a) tell how to begin and end a speech.

   (b) describe common faults of speech introductions.

   (c) compare speeches in the United States with those from other countries.

   (d) give ideas for speech topics.

_____ 2. A typographical aid used in this selection is

    (a) colored print.

    (b) graphics.

    (c) italic type.

    (d) enumeration.

_____ 3. In the United States and Western Europe, an apology generally is considered

    (a) an excellent way to begin a speech.

    (b) a compliment to the audience.

    (c) an excuse for a lack of competence or effectiveness.

    (d) a way of making the audience feel superior.

_____ 4. The word "irrelevant" (under the section "Don't Rely on Gimmicks") means

    (a) unrelated.

    (b) forceful.

    (c) interesting.

    (d) mistaken.

_____ 5. The problem with using a gimmick in a speech introduction is that

    (a) gimmicks usually don't gain the audience's attention.

    (b) the speaker using a gimmick may be seen as too arrogant.

    (c) gimmicks alert the audience that the speech should have been better.

    (d) the audience may resent being tricked into paying attention.

CHAPTER 11
Reading Graphic and Electronic Information

Directions: *Read the selection and the graphic that accompanies it, then answer the questions that follow.*

The success in improving humankind's most important crops has raised concern that we are becoming too reliant on too few crops (see Figure 8-25 below). Wheat responded to scientific yield enhancement so well that today humankind relies more on wheat than on any single crop in the past. If a new wheat disease suddenly appeared today, it could destroy a significant percentage of humankind's total food supply. Today humans rely on only 20 plant species for almost all of our food, but in the course of human history about 7,000 have been utilized, and at least 75,000 have edible parts. Many of them are superior to the plants cultivated today.

—adapted from *Introduction to Geography*, pp. 307-308

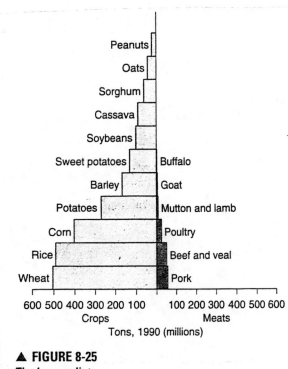

▲ **FIGURE 8-25**
The human diet.

_____ 1. The main point of this selection and its accompanying graphic is that

   (a) humans may be relying too much on too few crops.

   (b) humans have not succeeded in improving the most important crops.

   (c) a new wheat disease has suddenly appeared.

   (d) the plants cultivated today are superior to those grown in the past.

_____ 2. The type of graphic used in this selection is called a

    (a) pie chart.

    (b) flowchart.

    (c) pictogram.

    (d) bar graph.

_____ 3. The graphic indicates that, in 1990, humans consumed similar amounts of

    (a) wheat and pork.

    (b) beef and veal.

    (c) corn and goat.

    (d) peanuts and poultry.

_____ 4. The graphic indicates that, in 1990, humans consumed between 200 and 300 million tons of

    (a) corn.

    (b) potatoes.

    (c) barley.

    (d) sweet potatoes.

_____ 5. The word "utilized" (in the next to last sentence) means

    (a) removed.

    (b) destroyed.

    (c) used.

    (d) copied.

CHAPTER 12
Organizing and Remembering Information

Directions: *Read the selection and complete the time line below by matching the dates with the corresponding events; then answer the questions that follow.*

After the Transcontinental Treaty with Spain was ratified in February 1821, Americans began to settle in the fertile Texas plains by the thousands. As soon as the Mexican government began to restrict them, the Texans began to seek independence. In 1835 a series of skirmishes escalated into a full-scale rebellion. The Mexican president, Antonio Lopez de Santa Anna, marched north with 6000 soldiers to subdue the rebels. Late in February 1836 he reached San Antonio. A force of 187 men held the city, taking refuge behind the stout walls of a former mission called the Alamo. For ten days they beat off Santa Anna's assaults, inflicting terrible casualties on the attackers. Finally, on March 6, the Mexicans scaled the walls and killed everyone inside the Alamo.

Meanwhile, on March 2, 1836, Texas had declared its independence. Sam Houston, a former congressman and governor of Tennessee and an experienced Indian fighter, was placed in charge of the rebel army. For a time Houston retreated before Santa Anna's troops, who greatly outnumbered his own. Then, on April 21, 1836, Houston and his troops took a stand at the San Jacinto River, routing the Mexican army with cries of "Remember the Alamo!"

—adapted from *The American Nation,* pp. 329-330

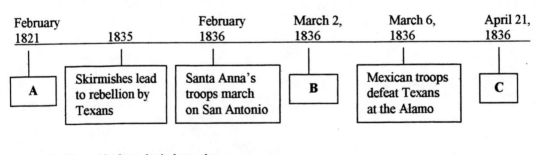

_____ 1. Texas declares its independence

_____ 2. Houston and his troops defeat the Mexican army

_____ 3. The Transcontinental Treaty with Spain is ratified

_____ 4. The purpose of this selection is to describe the

    (a) fight for Mexican independence from Spain.

    (b) negotiations for the land that later became Texas.

    (c) westward expansion of the United States.

    (d) events surrounding the battle of the Alamo.

_____ 5. The word "escalated" (in the third sentence) means

    (a) increased.

    (b) scaled back.

    (c) escaped.

    (d) retreated.

CHAPTER 13
Interpreting the Writer's Message and Purpose

Directions: *Read the selection, then answer the questions that follow.*

The Spanish and Portuguese brought terrible disaster to most American Indians. Having seen their gods mocked and their temples destroyed, many accepted Christianity as their only hope for survival, while toiling for their European masters. Some died from overwork, some were killed, and others simply languished as their cultures disintegrated. The most dangerous adversity was disease—European or African—to which American Indians had no immunities.

Epidemics arrived with Columbus and continued throughout the sixteenth century. Smallpox on Hispaniola in 1518 left only 1000 American Indians alive there. Cortés carried the pox to Mexico, where it raged while he fought his way out of Tenochtitlán. From Mexico the epidemic spread through Central America, reaching Peru in 1526. It killed the reigning emperor and helped start the civil war that facilitated Pizarro's conquest. Following these smallpox disasters in the 1540s and 1570s, a wave of measles, along with other successive epidemics, continued depleting the population.

--adapted from *Civilization Past & Present*, pp. 435-436

_____ 1. The purpose of this selection is to describe the

    (a) types of epidemics existed in Europe in the sixteenth century.

    (b) tragic impact of Europeans on American Indian life.

    (c) route that Columbus took in discovering the Americas.

    (d) conquest of Mexico and Peru.

_____ 2. The overall thought pattern of this selection is

    (a) definition.

    (b) comparison/contrast.

    (c) classification.

    (d) chronological order.

_____ 3. The tone of this selection is primarily

    (a) informal.

    (b) sympathetic.

    (c) humorous.

    (d) instructive.

_____ 4. An inference that can be made from the first paragraph is that

    (a) the American Indians were treated brutally by the European explorers.

    (b) most of the American Indians were glad to convert to Christianity.

    (c) the European explorers respected and admired the American Indian culture.

    (d) disease was not a problem for the American Indians.

_____ 5. A word in the last paragraph that has a negative connotation is

    (a) arrived.

    (b) carried.

    (c) raged.

    (d) reigning.

CHAPTER 14
Evaluating: Asking Critical Questions

Directions: *Read the selection, then answer the questions that follow.*

When people hear the term, "the Fed," they often think of Alan Greenspan, chairman of the Federal Reserve Board since 1987. Indeed, Dr. Greenspan is the most powerful economic policymaker in America, as evidenced by the way the economy hangs on his every word. However, the Fed is much more than Alan Greenspan. It has two basic and very important functions. The first is to ensure the orderly operation of the nation's banking system, which it does by bank supervision, check clearing, meeting currency needs, and lending funds to banks. The second is to control the nation's money supply, by setting the rules of the game for banks and by buying and selling government securities.

The Fed is a banker's bank. It provides the same services to banks that banks provide their own customers. All banks maintain deposit accounts, their "checking account," at the Fed. These accounts form the bulk of reserves and can be converted into currency at the bank's request. Thus, the Fed can meet the cash needs of banks. The Fed meets the credit or borrowing needs of banks as well. Any depository institution holding reserves at the Fed is entitled to borrow funds, but only for temporary and immediate credit needs.

The Fed also sets **reserve requirements**. American banks are required, by law, to hold reserve levels that meet a designated **required reserve ratio**—an amount of reserves that must be on hand to back bank deposits. A required reserve ratio of 5 percent means that banks must hold 5 cents for every dollar of deposits. Currently, the Fed requires that commercial banks maintain reserve ratios of 3 to 12 percent on checking accounts, and ratios of 0 to 3 percent on time and savings accounts.

> —adapted from *Essentials of Economics*, p. 186

_____ 1. The purpose of this selection is to

    (a) discuss Alan Greenspan's background and qualifications.

    (b) explain how the U.S. economy works.

    (c) describe the functions of the Fed.

    (d) compare the U.S. economy to the world economy.

_____ 2. The author supports the ideas in the selection primarily with

    (a) facts.

    (b) generalizations.

    (c) assumptions.

    (d) personal experience.

_____ 3. A sentence in the first paragraph that contains an opinion is the

    (a) second sentence.

    (b) fourth sentence.

    (c) fifth sentence.

    (d) last sentence.

_____ 4. The word "bulk" (in the second paragraph) is used in this selection to mean

    (a) weight.

    (b) main part.

    (c) awkward.

    (d) lump.

_____ 5. According to the selection, the Fed is responsible for

    (a) ensuring the orderly operation of the nation's banking system.

    (b) controlling the nation's money supply.

    (c) setting reserve requirements.

    (d) doing all of the above.

ANSWER KEY
PRACTICE TESTS
SET A

Chapter 1

1. c   2. b   3. d   4. a   5. d

Chapter 2

1. c   2. b   3. d   4. a   5. b

Chapter 3

1. a   2. b   3. a   4. d   5. c

Chapter 4

1. d   2. d   3. b   4. c   5. a

Chapter 5

1. b   2. c   3. d   4. a   5. b

Chapter 6

1. a   2. c   3. a   4. b   5. a

Chapter 7

1. a   2. b   3. d   4. b   5. a

Chapter 8

1. d   2. b   3. b   4. a   5. c

Chapter 9

1. d   2. a   3. a   4. c   5. b

Chapter 10

1. b   2. d   3. c   4. a   5. d

Chapter 11

1. a   2. d   3. d   4. b   5. c

Chapter 12

1. B   2. C   3. A   4. d   5. a

Chapter 13

1. b   2. d   3. b   4. a   5. c

Chapter 14

1. c   2. a   3. a   4. b   5. d

PRACTICE TESTS

SET B

CHAPTER 1
Successful Attitudes Toward Reading and Learning

Directions: *Read the selection, then answer the questions that follow.*

The performing arts have been a popular form of entertainment for thousands of years. For some areas, such as Branson, Missouri, they serve as primary tourism revenue generators; for other areas, such as Las Vegas, they serve as one more ingredient in the menu of attractions and entertainment that the area can boast of to interest visitors and encourage them to extend their stay. Live entertainment has always been a draw for travelers. For some it may be the opportunity to select from a wide variety of plays in London's theater district; for others, a chance to attend an opera performance or a concert featuring the newest entertainment idol.

The classical performing arts include theater (live stage plays, not the movies), ballet, opera, concerts, and the symphony. When combined they become "big business," generating over $8 billion a year in revenues in the United States alone. Contemporary performing arts include all these and more, such as stand-up and improvisational comedy, rock concerts, and even the band that is playing in your favorite local "hotspot." Performing arts entertainment, especially the classical forms, are frequently offered in locations such as concert halls, developed for the express purpose of showcasing the art form. The Kennedy Center in Washington, DC, is a well-known performing arts venue.

Theaters, concert halls, and other large-seating-capacity facilities exist in almost all cities throughout the world and each, no matter how plain or impressive, serves as a draw for visitors. Some, such as the Sydney Opera House, are even renowned as landmarks.

--adapted from *Tourism: The Business of Travel*, p. 164

_____ 1. The main point of this selection is that

    (a) the performing arts are a popular form of entertainment.

    (b) most people prefer live entertainment over movies.

    (c) the performing arts are a business.

    (d) every city should have a theater or concert hall.

_____ 2. According to the selection, the performing arts are the primary tourism revenue generator for

    (a) Branson, Missouri.

    (b) Las Vegas.

    (c) London.

    (d) Washington, DC.

_____ 3. The classical performing arts include all of the following *except*

    (a) stage plays.

    (b) the movies.

    (c) ballet.

    (d) opera.

_____ 4. The word "renowned" (in the last sentence) means

    (a) removed.

    (b) unknown.

    (c) measured.

    (d) famous.

_____ 5. If you found you were having difficulty comprehending this passage, you should

    (a) read aloud long or confusing sentences.

    (b) try to explain difficult ideas in your own words.

    (c) be sure you have chosen an appropriate place to study.

    (d) do all of the above.

CHAPTER 2
Using Context Clues

Directions: *Read the following selection, then use context to determine the meaning of the underlined words from the selection.*

In modern slang "Timbuktu" is a synonym for "nowhere," and few Americans even know that there really is such a place. In fact, Tombouctou is a city in Mali, <u>situated</u> on the Niger River where the river bends farthest north into the Sahara Desert. It plays no major role in today's world, but in past centuries it was a major urban center. The city was settled in 1087, and, as a major contact point between north and south, it <u>prospered</u> as a market for slaves, gold, and salt and as a point of departure for caravans traveling to North African coastal cities. From these cities Tombouctou's fame as a center of almost <u>mythical</u> riches spread around the Mediterranean. It was a religious center and it boasted a great university.

In the fifteenth century, however, Portuguese expeditions sailing around West Africa <u>outflanked</u> the trade routes on which Tombouctou depended. The city declined rapidly. It was captured by the Moroccans in 1591, and by the time the French captured it in 1893, it was little more than an extensive ruin. Today it is a small city of 10,000 people who live surrounded by few <u>remnants</u> of the city's former greatness.

--adapted from *Introduction to Geography*, p. 15

_____ 1. situated

    (a) located

    (b) promoted

    (c) created

    (d) departed

_____ 2. prospered

    (a) failed

    (b) changed

    (c) succeeded

    (d) attempted

_____ 3. mythical

    (a) legendary

    (b) hidden

    (c) terrible

    (d) playful

_____ 4. outflanked
    (a) raced
    (b) supplied
    (c) helped out
    (d) went around

_____ 5. remnants
    (a) residents
    (b) remains
    (c) profits
    (d) meetings

CHAPTER 3
Learning Word Parts

Directions: *Read the following selection, then use word parts to determine the meaning of the underlined words from the selection.*

There are several ways in which a drug can be taken into the body. Oral ingestion is the most common route of administration. Drugs that you swallow include tablets, capsules, and liquids. Another common form of drug administration is <u>intravenous</u> injection, which puts the chemical in its most concentrated form directly into the bloodstream. Effects will be felt within three minutes, making this route extremely effective in medical emergencies. Intramuscular injection, which is normally used to administer <u>antibiotics</u> and vaccinations, ensures a slow and consistent dispersion of the drug into the body tissues. <u>Subcutaneous</u> injection is commonly used for administration of local anesthetics and for insulin replacement therapy. A drug injected subcutaneously will <u>circulate</u> even more slowly than an intramuscularly injected drug because it takes longer to be absorbed into the bloodstream. Inunction introduces chemicals into the body through the skin; a common example of this method of drug administration is the small <u>adhesive</u> patches used to relieve motion sickness or to help people quit smoking.

--adapted from *Access to Health*, pp. 228-229

_____ 1. intravenous
  (a) through the mouth
  (b) into the veins
  (c) below the veins
  (d) above the veins

_____ 2. antibiotics
  (a) illegal drugs
  (b) drugs that stimulate growth
  (c) drugs that fight bacteria
  (d) recreational drugs

_____ 3. subcutaneous
  (a) on top of the skin
  (b) against the skin
  (c) away from the skin
  (d) under the skin

_____ 4. circulate
- (a) move around
- (b) listen to
- (c) repeat
- (d) take

_____ 5. adhesive
- (a) loose
- (b) backward
- (c) sticky
- (d) many

CHAPTER 4
Learning New Words

Directions: *Read the selection, then use a dictionary to answer the following questions about the underlined words.*

For criminal attorneys, one of the "lows" of the profession must surely be hearing the criticism "How can you defend such a person!?" The <u>implication</u> is that there must be something bad about criminal attorneys who <u>conscientiously</u> defend people who have committed <u>heinous</u> crimes. However, even if the defense attorney is convinced of a client's guilt, the ethics of the legal profession require that the client be defended to the best of the attorney's ability. Once a client is accepted, guilt or innocence should not influence the effort the attorney puts in on behalf of the client. Nor should personal distaste of a defendant be a reason for defense attorneys or prosecutors to <u>shirk</u> their professional obligations. A conscientious attorney may—indeed, should—turn down a case if he or she believes that personal distaste for a defendant would make it impossible to <u>mount</u> a proper defense.

--adapted from *Criminal Justice in America*, p. 362

_____ 1. The syllable that is most heavily stressed in "implication" is

    (a) im.

    (b) pli.

    (c) ca.

    (d) tion.

_____ 2. As a part of speech, the word "conscientiously" is

    (a) a noun.

    (b) a verb.

    (c) an adjective.

    (d) an adverb.

_____ 3. The best representation of the way to pronounce "heinous" is

    (a) high nus.

    (b) hay nus.

    (c) he in us.

    (d) hay nows.

_____ 4. The best synonym for the word "shirk" is

    (a) neglect.

    (b) respond.

    (c) move.

    (d) enjoy.

_____ 5. The definition of the word "mount" as it is used in this selection is

    (a) to climb or ascend.

    (b) a mountain or hill.

    (c) a setting for a jewel.

    (d) to prepare and set in motion.

CHAPTER 5
Reading as Thinking

Directions: *Read the selection, then answer the questions that follow.*

Market research data is often obtained through some form of *interactive instrument* in which the consumer responds to questions. The most common interactive instrument is a survey, a questionnaire asking participants about their beliefs or behaviors. Surveys can be administered in a variety of ways, each of which has its pros and cons.

1. *Mail surveys* are easy to administer and allow respondents to remain anonymous. On the downside, because the questionnaire is printed and mailed, researchers have little flexibility in the types of questions they can ask and little control over the circumstances under which the respondent is answering them. Mail surveys also take a long time to get back to the company and are likely to have a much lower response rate than other types of surveys because people tend to ignore them.

2. *Telephone surveys* consist of a brief phone conversation in which an interviewer reads a short list of questions to the respondent. One problem with this approach is that the growth of telemarketing has eroded the willingness of many consumers to participate in phone surveys. In addition, the respondent may not feel comfortable speaking directly to an interviewer, especially about a sensitive subject. Finally, many people use answering machines to screen calls, further reducing the response rate.

3. *Face-to-face surveys*, in which an interviewer asks questions of a respondent by going door-to-door, used to be a common way to collect data. However, this practice has declined in recent years due to rising costs and security concerns. Today's face-to-face interviews typically occur in a "mall-intercept" study in which researchers recruit shoppers in malls or other public areas. In addition to being more expensive than mail or phone surveys, respondents may be reluctant to answer personal questions face-to-face.

4. *On-line surveys* are growing in popularity as more consumers are getting hooked up to the Internet. This technology is still in its infancy and many questions linger about the quality of responses the firm will receive—particularly because (as with mail and phone interviews) no one can be really sure who is typing in the responses.

--adapted from *Marketing: Real People, Real Choices*, pp. 130-131

_____ 1. The purpose of this selection is to

    (a) describe the questions that are asked on surveys.

    (b) encourage companies to use surveys for market research.

    (c) compare surveys to other types of market research.

    (d) describe the types of surveys that are used for market research.

_____ 2. To preview this selection you should read

    (a) the entire passage through quickly.

    (b) only the first paragraph.

    (c) the items in boldface.

    (d) only the last paragraph.

_____ 3. The most useful guide question for this selection would be

    (a) Who conducts surveys?

    (b) Are surveys a good way to obtain market research data?

    (c) What type of survey is used most frequently?

    (d) What are the advantages and disadvantages of different types of surveys?

_____ 4. The word "eroded" (under the heading "Telephone surveys") means

    (a) decreased.

    (b) interested.

    (c) improved.

    (d) demanded.

_____ 5. The typographical aids used in this selection include

    (a) italics.

    (b) boldfaced type.

    (c) enumeration (listing).

    (d) all of the above.

CHAPTER 6
Understanding Sentences

Directions: *Read the selection, then answer the questions that follow.*

The story of American party struggle is primarily the story of two major parties, but third parties are a regular feature of American politics and occasionally attract the public's attention. Third parties come in three basic varieties. First are parties that promote certain causes—either a controversial single issue (prohibition of alcoholic beverages, for example) or an extreme ideological position such as socialism or libertarianism. Second are splinter parties, which are offshoots of a major party. Teddy Roosevelt's Progressives in 1912, Strom Thurmond's States' Righters in 1948, and George Wallace's American Independents in 1968 all claimed they did not get a fair hearing from Republicans or Democrats and thus formed their own new parties. Finally, some third parties are merely an extension of a popular individual with presidential aspirations. Both John Anderson in 1980 and Ross Perot in 1992 and 1996 offered voters who were dissatisfied with the Democratic and Republican nominees another option.

--adapted from *Government in America*, pp. 262-263

_____ 1. The purpose of this selection is to
   (a) describe the characteristics of the two major parties.
   (b) describe the three basic types of third parties.
   (c) explain why most people belong to one of the two major parties.
   (d) convince voters to consider third-party candidates.

_____ 2. The coordinating conjunction in the first sentence is
   (a) is.
   (b) primarily.
   (c) but.
   (d) occasionally.

_____ 3. Teddy Roosevelt's Progressive Party was an example of the type of third party formed as
   (a) an offshoot of a major party.
   (b) an extension of a popular individual who wanted to be president.
   (c) a way to promote an extreme ideological position.
   (d) a way to demonstrate support for a controversial issue.

_____ 4. The best synonym for the word "aspirations" (in the next to last sentence) is

    (a) agreements.

    (b) arguments.

    (c) ambitions.

    (d) abuses.

_____ 5. The best paraphrase for the last sentence is

    (a) Both John Anderson and Ross Perot offered voters Democratic and Republican nominees.

    (b) Voters unhappy with the Democratic and Republican nominees were given another choice by John Anderson in 1980 and by Ross Perot in 1992 and 1996.

    (c) In 1980 and in 1992 and in 1996 voters were given another option.

    (d) Both John Anderson in 1980 and Ross Perot in 1992 and 1996 were dissatisfied with the Democratic and Republican nominees.

CHAPTER 7
Understanding Paragraphs: Topics, Stated Main Ideas, and Implied Main Ideas

Directions: *Read the selection, then answer the questions that follow.*

Tornadoes are intense columns of rising air, usually associated with thunderstorms. As the air rises, it creates a partial vacuum (an area of very low pressure) that draws air in toward it. As this air is drawn in, it creates a swirling vortex, much like the swirling motion of water as it drains out of a sink. As the air swirls, it gains tremendous speed, sometimes exceeding 185 miles per hour. This vortex usually moves horizontally, sometimes touching the ground and sometimes rising above it, leaving an erratic and usually very narrow path of destruction.

Most tornadoes occur in one of two circulation patterns: in association with intense thunderstorms embedded in hurricanes, and along especially strong cold fronts in the midlatitudes. The south-central United States has the greatest frequency of tornadoes of any place in the world. In the United States they occur mostly in spring and early summer, when contrasts between cold, dry continental air and moist, humid air from the Gulf of Mexico are greatest. Such conditions create cells of rapidly rising air, including very intense thunderstorms and, sometimes, tornadoes.

--adapted from *Introduction to Geography*, p. 62

_____ 1. The main idea of the first paragraph is that tornadoes

    (a) consist of a swirling vortex of air.

    (b) may have wind speeds in excess of 185 miles per hour.

    (c) are highly destructive.

    (d) move horizontally.

_____ 2. The topic of the second paragraph is

    (a) thunderstorms.

    (b) hurricanes.

    (c) tornadoes.

    (d) seasons.

_____ 3. The word "erratic" (in the first paragraph) means

    (a) mistaken.

    (b) irregular.

    (c) unnatural.

    (d) mild.

_____ 4. In the United States, tornadoes occur mostly in

    (a) spring and early summer.

    (b) late summer.

    (c) fall.

    (d) winter.

_____ 5. According to the selection, the greatest frequency of tornadoes occurs

    (a) outside the United States.

    (b) in the Gulf of Mexico.

    (c) in the south-central United States.

    (d) in South America.

CHAPTER 8
Understanding Paragraphs: Supporting Details and Transitions

Directions: *Read the selection, then answer the questions that follow.*

Ecotourism, sometimes called "green tourism," has evolved in reaction to the problems of mass tourism. Ecotourism is a form of tourism that emphasizes the need to minimize environmental impact and ensure that host communities gain the greatest economic and cultural benefits possible. The goal is to integrate tourism development into a broader range of values and social concerns.

Mass tourism, in contrast to ecotourism, tends to strain the environment through the development of more and more superstructure and the increasing wear and tear from tourists. Building hotels, restaurants, roads, and airports can cause serious problems for an area's environment. For example, the construction of ski resorts in the Alps has led to mudslides and landslides that are damaging the mountainsides. How do individuals threaten the environment? One way is simply by blazing trails while walking through nature. One person walking through a wilderness area may not have any significant impact on the area, but 10,000 people within a short period certainly will. The simple action of trampling grass multiplied by 10,000 can lead to erosion of land. For example, several of New York State's Adirondack Mountain peaks are now bare due to hiker traffic.

--adapted from *Tourism: The Business of Travel*, pp. 253-255

_____ 1. The purpose of this selection is to

    (a) list tourist locations that encourage ecotourism.

    (b) describe the harmful effects of mass tourism and the movement toward ecotourism.

    (c) describe the causes of mudslides and landslides in the Alps.

    (d) explain how animals and plants are affected by tourism.

_____ 2. In the second paragraph, the transitional phrase that indicates that a different idea is going to be discussed is

    (a) in contrast.

    (b) For example.

    (c) One way.

    (d) can lead to.

_____ 3. The word "integrate" (in the first paragraph) means

    (a) separate.

    (b) educate.

    (c) blend.

    (d) demand.

_____ 4. The last sentence of the selection provides a

    (a) topic sentence.

    (b) minor detail.

    (c) key detail.

    (d) main idea.

_____ 5. According to the selection, several of the peaks in New York State's Adirondack Mountains are bare because of

    (a) hotel construction.

    (b) mudslides and landslides.

    (c) ecotourism.

    (d) hiker traffic.

CHAPTER 9
Following the Author's Thought Patterns

Directions: *Read the selection, then answer the questions that follow.*

The study of individual and collective aging processes, known as gerontology, explores the reasons for aging and the ways in which people cope with this process. Gerontologists have identified several types of age-related characteristics that should be used to determine where a person is in terms of life-stage development:

- *Biological age* refers to the relative age or condition of the person's organs and body systems. Does the person who is 70 years old have the level of physiological functioning that might be expected of someone in that age group? Arthritis and other chronic conditions often speed up the aging process.

- *Psychological age* refers to a person's adaptive capacities, such as coping abilities and intelligence, and to the person's awareness of his or her individual capabilities and general ability to adapt to a given situation. Psychological age is typically assessed on the basis of everyday behavior, personal interviews, or tests.

- *Social age* refers to a person's habits and roles relative to society's expectations. People in a particular life stage usually share similar tastes in music, television shows, and politics. Whereas rap music often appeals to teenagers and people in their twenties, it may repel middle-aged and older people.

- *Legal age* is probably the most common definition of age in the United States. Legal age is based on chronological years and is used to determine such things as voting rights, driving privileges, drinking age, eligibility for Social Security payments, and other rights and obligations.

- *Functional age* refers to the ways in which people compare to others of a similar age. Heart rate, skin thickness, hearing, and other individual characteristics are analyzed and compared. A person's ability to perform a given job-related task is also part of this assessment. It is difficult to separate functional aging from many of the other types of aging, particularly chronological and biological aging.

　　　　　--adapted from *Access to Health*, pp. 517-518

_____ 1. The main point of this selection is that

    (a) gerontology is the study of the aging process.

    (b) many people have trouble coping with the effects of aging.

    (c) people are often discriminated against because of their age.

    (d) a person's age can be described according to several types of age-related characteristics.

_____ 2. The overall thought pattern of this selection is

    (a) comparison/contrast.

    (b) chronological order.

    (c) classification.

    (d) cause/effect.

_____ 3. Of the following words or phrases from the selection, the one that suggests the overall thought pattern of this selection is

    (a) whereas.

    (b) types of age-related characteristics.

    (c) relative.

    (d) explores the reasons.

_____ 4. The word "repel" (under the heading "Social age") means

    (a) offend.

    (b) attract.

    (c) criticize.

    (d) review.

_____ 5. A person's social age refers to his or her

    (a) coping abilities and intelligence.

    (b) physiological condition.

    (c) habits and roles relative to society's expectations.

    (d) ability to perform a given job-related task.

CHAPTER 10
Reading Textbook Chapters

Directions: *Read the selection, then answer the questions that follow.*

Psychologist Jean Piaget (1896-1980) described four major stages of cognitive development. Each period is governed by a different type of logic and includes many substages, with key characteristics. The periods overlap slightly, and they may occur at different ages for different children.

The infant's experience begins in the *sensorimotor period*, from birth to age 2. In the early stages of this period, the infant does not yet understand that objects (including people) continue to exist even when they cannot be seen. For example, a rattle dropped over the side of a high chair is quickly forgotten—and more than forgotten: out of sight means not just out of mind but out of existence! By the end of the sensorimotor period, the toddler understands that objects exist even when they are no longer perceived.

Once out of the sensorimotor period, the child enters the *preoperational period*, from age 2 until age 7. Armed with the ability to form mental representations, children in this period are able to think about objects and events that are not immediately present. As a result, they can imitate actions that occurred in the past and can engage in fantasy play.

By the end of the preoperational period, about age 7, children develop the ability to take another person's point of view. This ability is linked to the fact that they can now perform **concrete operations** and are able to grasp concepts such as length, width, volume, and time, and to understand various mental operations such as those involved in simple arithmetic. This *period of concrete operations* takes place between ages 7 and 11.

The ability to reason abstractly emerges around the ages of 11 or 12, at the onset of what Piaget termed the *period of formal operations*. Rather than simply understanding the logic of "what is," as occurs with concrete operations, the child is now able to imagine the possibilities of "what could be." **Formal operations** allow children to engage in abstract thinking, to think about "what-would-happen-if" situations, and to think about the possible outcomes of an act by being able to list alternatives in advance and consider each in turn.

--adapted from *Psychology: The Brain, the Person, the World*, pp. 400–402

_____ 1. All of the following statements about this selection are true *except*

    (a) Jean Piaget identified four stages of cognitive development.

    (b) every child goes through each stage at exactly the same age.

    (c) children understand by age 2 that objects exist even when they are no longer perceived.

    (d) children develop the ability to take another person's point of view around age 7.

_____ 2. Piaget called the first stage of cognitive development the

   (a) primary period.

   (b) sensorimotor period.

   (c) preoperational period.

   (d) period of concrete operations.

_____ 3. The overall thought pattern of this selection is

   (a) cause/effect.

   (b) comparison/contrast.

   (c) classification.

   (d) illustration/example.

_____ 4. The word "armed" (in the third paragraph) is used in this selection to mean

   (a) guarded.

   (b) changed.

   (c) dangerous.

   (d) equipped.

_____ 5. Children become able to consider "what-would-happen-if" situations in the

   (a) sensorimotor period.

   (b) preoperational period.

   (c) period of concrete operations.

   (d) period of formal operations.

CHAPTER 11
Reading Graphic and Electronic Information

Directions: *Read the selection and the graphic that accompanies it, then answer the questions that follow.*

Modern American society depends on the availability of abundant energy. Producing the amounts of energy necessary to retain Americans' standard of living and accustomed patterns of life while at the same time preserving the environment has become increasingly difficult, however. Energy issues continually present thorny problems for policymakers to resolve, and government is constantly involved in battles concerning what forms of energy the country should be producing, and from what sources.

Once Americans used wood, animals, water, and people power for energy. Today, most of the nation's energy comes from coal, oil, and natural gas (see Figure 19.4 below). Americans search continually for new and more efficient sources of energy, both to increase supplies and to reduce pollution.

—adapted from *Government in America*, pp. 631-632

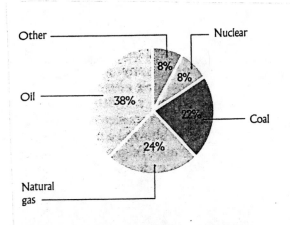

Figure 19.4
Sources of America's Energy

SOURCE: U.S. Bureau of the Census, *Statistical Abstract of the United States, 1998* (Washington, DC: U.S. Government Printing Office, 1998), 588.

_____ 1. The purpose of this selection and its accompanying graphic is to
  (a) describe America's dependence on energy.
  (b) identify alternative sources of energy.
  (c) describe how coal causes pollution.
  (d) explain the government's energy policies.

_____ 2. The type of graphic used in this selection is called a

   (a) multiple bar graph.

   (b) linear graph.

   (c) flowchart.

   (d) pie chart.

_____ 3. The word "abundant" (in the first sentence) means

   (a) natural.

   (b) plentiful.

   (c) expensive.

   (d) local.

_____ 4. The graphic indicates that the energy source that Americans rely on most is

   (a) nuclear.

   (b) coal.

   (c) oil.

   (d) natural gas.

_____ 5. According to the graphic, the percentage of the nation's energy that comes from sources other than coal, oil, nuclear, or natural gas is

   (a) 0%.

   (b) 8%.

   (c) 16%.

   (d) 22%.

CHAPTER 12
Organizing and Remembering Information

Directions: *Read the selection and complete the outline in the box by answering the questions that follow.*

A firm seeking to sell a product in a foreign market has three choices: sell the same product in the new market, modify it for the market, or develop a brand-new product for the foreign market. Let's take a closer look at each possibility.

- A *straight extension strategy* retains the same product for domestic and foreign markets. Coca-Cola sells the same formula in every country, and Gillette offers the same razor blades everywhere.

- A *product adaptation strategy* recognizes that in many cases people in different cultures have different product preferences. These differences can be subtle, yet important. That explains why Kellogg, which sells identical versions of its Corn Flakes and Rice Krispies brands in the United States and Europe, had to remove the green "loops" from Froot Loops after research showed that Europeans felt they looked too artificial. In other cases, products must be adapted because living conditions or customs require different designs. For example, because the British are avid purchasers of frozen foods, they insist on refrigerators with 60 percent freezer space.

- A *product invention strategy* means that a company develops a new product as it expands to foreign markets. In some cases, a product invention strategy takes the form of *backward invention*. The firm may need to offer a less complex product than it sells elsewhere, such as a manually operated sewing machine or a hand-powered clothes washer to people without access to a reliable source of electricity.

> --adapted from *Marketing: Real People, Real Choices*, p. 107

```
                    Outline: Selling a Product in a Foreign Market

  I.      Straight Extension Strategy
          A. Same product for _____(X)_____
  II.     Product Adaptation Strategy
          A. Products modified because of cultural preferences
             1. Kellogg's Froot Loops
          B. Products adapted because of _____(Y)_____
             1. Refrigerators for British
  III.    Product _____(Z)_____ Strategy
          A. New product developed for foreign markets
          B. Backward invention
```

_____ 1. The best word or phrase to replace the (X) above is

    (a) Coca-Cola.

    (b) Gillette.

    (c) razor blades.

    (d) domestic and foreign markets.

_____ 2. The best word or phrase to replace the (Y) above is

    (a) cultural preferences.

    (b) living conditions or customs.

    (c) research.

    (d) avid purchasers.

_____ 3. The best word or phrase to replace the (Z) above is

    (a) extension.

    (b) adaptation.

    (c) invention.

    (d) develop.

_____ 4. The main point of the selection is that

    (a) companies must develop new products whenever they enter a foreign market.

    (b) people in the United States and Europe like the same products.

    (c) people in the United States and Europe like completely different products.

    (d) companies that want to sell products in foreign markets have three options.

_____ 5. The word "subtle" (under the heading "A product adaptation strategy") means

    (a) ideal.

    (b) not obvious.

    (c) dramatic.

    (d) unimportant.

CHAPTER 13
Interpreting the Writer's Message and Purpose

Directions: *Read the selection, then answer the questions that follow.*

The automobile made life more mobile. It changed recreational patterns and family life. It created a generation of tinkerers and amateur mechanics and explorers. In addition, it profoundly affected the way Americans thought. It gave them a freedom never before imagined. The owner of the most rickety jalopy could travel further, faster, and far more comfortably than a king in a gilded coach.

These benefits were real and priceless. But cars came to have a symbolic significance that was equally important: They gave their owners a feeling of power and status similar to that which owning a horse gave to a medieval knight. According to some authorities the typical American cared more about owning an automobile than a house.

In time there were undesirable, even dangerous results of the automotive revolution: roadside scenery disfigured by billboards, gas stations, and other enterprises aimed at satisfying the traveler's needs; horrendous traffic jams; soaring accident rates; air pollution. All these disadvantages were noticed during the 1920s, but in the springtime of the new industry they were discounted. The automobile seemed an unalloyed blessing—part toy, part tool, part symbol of American freedom, prosperity, and individualism.

--adapted from *The American Nation*, p. 712

_____ 1. The main point of this selection is that

   (a) the disadvantages of owning an automobile outweigh the benefits.

   (b) billboards have spoiled the scenery along American roads.

   (c) many people view their automobiles as toys.

   (d) the automobile had a dramatic effect on American life.

_____ 2. The tone of this selection is primarily

   (a) angry.

   (b) nostalgic.

   (c) humorous.

   (d) disapproving.

_____ 3. One example of descriptive language in the selection is

  (a) "The automobile made life more mobile."

  (b) ". . . more comfortably than a king in a gilded coach."

  (c) ". . . the typical American cared more about owning an automobile than a house."

  (d) "All these disadvantages were noticed during the 1920s."

_____ 4. One word from the third paragraph that has a positive connotation is

  (a) automotive.

  (b) disfigured.

  (c) springtime.

  (d) jams.

_____ 5. The word "unalloyed" (in the last sentence) means

  (a) pure or unqualified.

  (b) having to do with metal.

  (c) dangerous or undesirable.

  (d) imaginary.

CHAPTER 14
Evaluating: Asking Critical Questions

Directions: *Read the selection, then answer the questions that follow.*

One sure sign that the Christmas season has begun is the annual crop of articles about holiday depression, which appear as reliably as department store Santas. This has led to the widespread belief that the holidays breed serious emotional troubles, and even that the suicide rate peaks around December 25. Are the holidays "public health hazards"?

No, according to Dr. James Hillard of the University of Cincinnati, who examined these assumptions about holiday misery and found that suicides do not occur more frequently around Christmas, nor are people more likely to suffer from severe depression (as measured by hospital admissions for psychiatric problems). In fact, December has a comparatively low rate of suicides and other psychiatric emergencies. The suicide rate usually does not begin to rise until January and then peaks in April or May.

Why is there this gap between belief and reality? Two common by-products of holiday celebrations are stress and anxiety. People should not spend more than they can afford, or eat and drink too much at holiday gatherings; by doing so they only add to their own stress and anxiety. The holidays also disrupt most people's normal patterns of sleep, exercise, and work. Even for the relatively well adjusted, life is frenetic—the shops are mobbed and traffic is snarled. On top of that, many people suffer from seasonal affective disorder (SAD) due largely to the lack of sunlight during the short days this time of year.

--adapted from *HealthStyles: Decisions for Living Well,* p. 80

_____ 1. The purpose of this selection is to

    (a) explain why people become suicidal during the holidays.

    (b) describe seasonal affective disorder (SAD).

    (c) discuss assumptions and facts about holiday depression.

    (d) compare suicides to other psychiatric emergencies.

_____ 2. The first sentence of the second paragraph is an example of

    (a) a generalization.

    (b) an informed opinion.

    (c) an assumption.

    (d) a statistic.

_____ 3. The sentence in the last paragraph that contains a value judgment is the

    (a) first sentence.

    (b) second sentence.

    (c) third sentence.

    (d) fourth sentence.

_____ 4. The word "frenetic" (in the next to last sentence) means

    (a) hectic.

    (b) boring.

    (c) pleasant.

    (d) depressing.

_____ 5. According to this selection, the holiday season commonly leads to increases in all of the following _except_

    (a) stress.

    (b) anxiety.

    (c) disruptions of normal sleep patterns.

    (d) suicide rates.

ANSWER KEY
PRACTICE TESTS
SET B

Chapter 1

1. a   2. a   3. b   4. d   5. d

Chapter 2

1. a   2. c   3. a   4. d   5. b

Chapter 3

1. b   2. c   3. d   4. a   5. c

Chapter 4

1. c   2. d   3. b   4. a   5. d

Chapter 5

1. d   2. c   3. d   4. a   5. d

Chapter 6

1. b   2. c   3. a   4. c   5. b

Chapter 7

1. a   2. c   3. b   4. a   5. c

Chapter 8

1. b 　　 2. a 　　 3. c 　　 4. b 　　 5. d

Chapter 9

1. d 　　 2. c 　　 3. b 　　 4. a 　　 5. c

Chapter 10

1. b 　　 2. b 　　 3. c 　　 4. d 　　 5. d

Chapter 11

1. a 　　 2. d 　　 3. b 　　 4. c 　　 5. b

Chapter 12

1. d 　　 2. b 　　 3. c 　　 4. d 　　 5. b

Chapter 13

1. d 　　 2. b 　　 3. b 　　 4. c 　　 5. a

Chapter 14

1. c 　　 2. b 　　 3. c 　　 4. a 　　 5. d

PART THREE

VOCABULARY QUIZZES

VOCABULARY QUIZ 1

Directions: *Match each definition to the word part it defines.*

_____	1. anti	(a) different
_____	2. auto	(b) time
_____	3. bio	(c) write
_____	4. chron	(d) word, study
_____	5. eu	(e) life
_____	6. graph	(f) opposite
_____	7. hetero	(g) measure
_____	8. homo	(h) good, well
_____	9. log	(i) self
_____	10. meter	(j) same, like

VOCABULARY QUIZ 2

Directions: *From the list below, select the proper word part so that the appropriate word is formed.*

(a) bio   (b) eu   (c) log   (d) chron   (e) graph

(f) auto   (g) anti   (h) hetero   (i) meter   (j) homo

_____ 1. College students have more _____nomy than high school students, therefore they must learn to be more responsible.

_____ 2. The old man appears to be _____social; he rarely leaves his house or talks to his family.

_____ 3. The people at the party were a _____geneous group; they all appeared to enjoy the same music and activities.

_____ 4. The new houses in our development are quite _____geneous in design, with ranch, split-level, and Victorian types all represented.

_____ 5. Susan felt _____phoric about her job promotion.

_____ 6. The _____sphere is the part of the earth's crust, waters and atmosphere that supports living organisms.

_____ 7. The author provided an epi_____ at the end of her book to explain what happens to her family.

_____ 8. A hygro_____ measures the water vapor content in the atmosphere.

_____ 9. The study of handwriting is known as _____ology.

_____ 10. The newly married couple started a diary to provide a _____icle of their life together to give to their children.

VOCABULARY QUIZ 3

Directions: *Match each definition to the word part it defines.*

_____ 1. uni		(a) carry
_____ 2. voc		(b) to see
_____ 3. port		(c) land, earth
_____ 4. therm		(d) heat
_____ 5. terr		(e) across
_____ 6. cred		(f) feeling
_____ 7. trans		(g) believe
_____ 8. un		(h) not
_____ 9. path		(i) one
_____ 10. vis		(j) call, voice

VOCABULARY QUIZ 4

Directions: *From the list below, select the proper word part so that the appropriate word is formed.*

(a) dict   (b) terr   (c) trans   (d) uni   (e) vis

(f) vert   (g) therm   (h) un   (i) ver   (j) voc

_____ 1. The instant replay provided _____ification that our team had won the football game.

_____ 2. The _____ain was too rocky for planting our vegetables.

_____ 3. Even though the expensive vase was dropped it remained _____broken.

_____ 4. The interviewer asked the potential employee what he en_____ioned doing in five years.

_____ 5. The travelers con_____ed Canadian currency to American dollars.

_____ 6. The minister's in_____ation began the morning services.

_____ 7. All of the children in the marching band were required to wear _____forms.

_____ 8. Many students are able to pre_____ their exam grades.

_____ 9. When I _____planted the tree to a different location, it grew much bigger.

_____ 10. _____odynamics deals with the connection between heat and mechanical energy.

VOCABULARY QUIZ 5

Directions: *Match each definition to the word part it defines.*

_____	1. extra	(a) not
_____	2. in	(b) out
_____	3. anti	(c) beyond
_____	4. non	(d) false
_____	5. pre	(e) equal
_____	6. ex	(f) against
_____	7. pseudo	(g) around
_____	8. mal	(h) evil
_____	9. circum	(i) put into
_____	10. equi	(j) before

Name: _____ Date: _____ Section: _____

VOCABULARY QUIZ 6

Directions: *From the list below, select the proper word part so that the appropriate word is formed.*

(a) de　　　(b) en　　　(c) ex　　　(d) mal　　　(e) circum

(f) extra　　(g) dis　　　(h) in　　　(i) pseudo　　(j) equ

_____ 1. Since the crime was committed without _____ice, the sentence was not as severe.

_____ 2. The magician tried to _____entangle himself from the ropes during his performance.

_____ 3. Congress _____acted the bill after it was rejected twice.

_____ 4. Areas next to the earth's _____ator have extremely hot temperatures.

_____ 5. The student teacher was _____competent; therefore, she was not hired for full-time employment.

_____ 6. The explorer _____navigated the world.

_____ 7. The writer chose a _____nym rather than use his real name.

_____ 8. New cars _____preciate in value as soon as they are driven off the lot.

_____ 9. During his asthma attack, the boy had difficulty _____haling.

_____ 10. The Academy Awards are a wonderful _____vaganza to witness in person.

VOCABULARY QUIZ 7

Directions: *Using context clues, select the best meaning for the italicized word.*

_____ 1. We keep candles in the house to *avert* being left in the dark during power failures.

    (a) prevent

    (b) ensure

    (c) accommodate

    (d) begin

_____ 2. To *compel* the man to hand over his wallet, the mugger said he had a gun.

    (a) avoid

    (b) delight

    (c) force

    (d) finish

_____ 3. All of the movies I wanted to rent were taken, so as an *alternative* I went home and read a book.

    (a) command

    (b) design

    (c) assignment

    (d) another option

_____ 4. Student journalists are taught how to be *concise* when writing in a limited space.

    (a) peaceful

    (b) clear and brief

    (c) proper

    (d) wordy

_____ 5. There should be more *drastic* penalties to stop people from littering.

    (a) dirty

    (b) suitable

    (c) extreme

    (d) pleasant

_____ 6. To *fortify* his diet while weightlifting, the body builder took twelve vitamins a day.

   (a) suggest

   (b) strengthen

   (c) avoid

   (d) approve of

_____ 7. The cat and her newborn kittens had to be *isolated* from the family dog after he tried to attack them.

   (a) combined

   (b) heated up

   (c) separated

   (d) rejected

_____ 8. On their wedding anniversary, the husband and wife *reminisced* about how they first met.

   (a) gathered

   (b) remembered

   (c) traveled

   (d) forgot

_____ 9. During the Christmas season, many people use decorative lights to *illuminate* their homes.

   (a) loose

   (b) avoid

   (c) light up

   (d) suitable

_____ 10. The baby birds needed a place of *refuge* from the winter storm.

   (a) shelter

   (b) rejection

   (c) building

   (d) separate

VOCABULARY QUIZ 8

Directions: *Using context clues, select the best meaning for the italicized word.*

_____ 1. Mike's efforts to buy a car were *futile*, so he continued to ride his bike to work.

    (a) helpful

    (b) useless

    (c) necessary

    (d) careless

_____ 2. Janice was *persistent* in asking her mother to buy a new car, so she finally gave in and bought one.

    (a) stubborn

    (b) lazy

    (c) clever

    (d) friendly

_____ 3. Being extremely thin has become an *obsession* for many teenage girls.

    (a) behavior

    (b) compulsion

    (c) punishment

    (d) separation

_____ 4. Tim and his father are not speaking to one another, so I *infer* that they had a fight.

    (a) offer

    (b) reject

    (c) conclude

    (d) answer

_____ 5. Getting our car fixed after the accident was an *ordeal*.

    (a) good time

    (b) change

    (c) unclear

    (d) painful experience

_____ 6. The teenager died from drinking a *lethal* amount of alcohol during a party.

- (a) harmless
- (b) moderate
- (c) deadly
- (d) excessive

_____ 7. Monica let a few weeks *elapse* before returning her ex-boyfriend's phone call.

- (a) separate
- (b) pass
- (c) slow down
- (d) speed up

_____ 8. Gorillas can *convey* messages to humans through gestures and sounds.

- (a) invent
- (b) allow
- (c) communicate
- (d) approve

_____ 9. The veterinarian gave the puppies vitamins to *stimulate* their appetite.

- (a) arouse
- (b) confuse
- (c) stop
- (d) delay

_____ 10. The picture of the woman had *universal* appeal so the promoters used it in their advertising campaign.

- (a) humorous
- (b) including everyone
- (c) local
- (d) doubtful

VOCABULARY QUIZ 9

Directions: *Using context clues, select the best meaning for the italicized word.*

_____ 1. After visiting the dark cave, it was difficult to make the *transition* into the sunlight.

    (a) purchase

    (b) invention

    (c) change

    (d) repetition

_____ 2. My *conservative* grandparents were disappointed when I served a vegetarian meal for Thanksgiving.

    (a) resisting change

    (b) opinionated

    (c) not definite

    (d) understanding

_____ 3. The fact that Tim was ten years older than Sandy was enough to *deter* her from dating him.

    (a) damage

    (b) refuse

    (c) prevent

    (d) dislike

_____ 4. The professor *denounced* the student for cheating and then failed him for the semester.

    (a) introduced

    (b) condemned

    (c) changed

    (d) complimented

_____ 5. Since Antonia was not in good physical condition, she could not *sustain* the aerobics workout.

    (a) easily affected

    (b) delay

    (c) resist

    (d) withstand

6. The reward for turning in the lost wallet far *surpassed* what John thought it would be.

   (a) undermined

   (b) opposed

   (c) went beyond

   (d) wore away

7. The conference on cultural *diversity* attracted people from all over the world.

   (a) obvious

   (b) variety

   (c) profitable

   (d) support

8. I only made *tentative* plans to go to the movies Saturday night.

   (a) not definite

   (b) obvious

   (c) certain

   (d) support

9. Because the infant was so small, the doctors gave her vitamins to *supplement* her diet.

   (a) replace

   (b) stop

   (c) add to

   (d) weaken

10. Ross decided to *compensate* his son for driving him to work all week while his car was being repaired.

   (a) receive

   (b) win out

   (c) change

   (d) pay

VOCABULARY QUIZ 10

Directions: *Using context clues, select the best meaning for the italicized word.*

_____ 1. The boxer hit his opponent with such *impact* that he broke his jaw.

    (a) strike

    (b) threat

    (c) force

    (d) weakness

_____ 2. Most people favor new drunk driving laws, but many of them do not *endorse* vehicle confiscation.

    (a) stop

    (b) suggest

    (c) start

    (d) support

_____ 3. When Jim decided to drop out of high school, he didn't realize his decision would be an *obstacle* to getting a good job.

    (a) barrier

    (b) assistance

    (c) rejection

    (d) advantage

_____ 4. The raccoons were a *menace* to our backyard. They ate our tomato plants and dug holes in the grass.

    (a) help

    (b) barrier

    (c) threat

    (d) force

_____ 5. My computer *deleted* two programs that I can no longer purchase.

    (a) repeated

    (b) damaged

    (c) removed

    (d) delayed

_____ 6. The team's *morale* was destroyed when it lost the playoff game.

  (a) principle

  (b) spirit

  (c) majority

  (d) opposition

_____ 7. The judge was *lenient* on the teenager since it was his first offense.

  (a) not strict

  (b) heavy

  (c) forceful

  (d) biased

_____ 8. A good teacher must remain *impartial* in order to run a successful classroom.

  (a) not whole

  (b) strict

  (c) judgmental

  (d) not biased

_____ 9. The woman's behavior was so *erratic* that she couldn't stay employed for more than a week.

  (a) friendly

  (b) not consistent

  (c) rejected

  (d) objected

_____ 10. Oversleeping is not a *legitimate* excuse for missing class.

  (a) obvious

  (b) profitable

  (c) acceptable

  (d) pragmatic

ANSWER KEY
Vocabulary Quizzes

Quiz 1

1. ' f	2. i	3. e	4. b	5. h
6. c	7. a	8. j	9. d	10. g

Quiz 2

1. f	2. g	3. j	4. h	5. b
6. a	7. e	8. i	9. c	10. d

Quiz 3

1. i	2. j	3. a	4. d	5. c
6. g	7. e	8. h	9. f	10. b

Quiz 4

1. i	2. b	3. h	4. e	5. f
6. j	7. d	8. a	9. c	10. g

Quiz 5

1. c	2. i	3. f	4. a	5. j
6. b	7. d	8. h	9. g	10. e

Quiz 6

1. d	2. g	3. b	4. j	5. h
6. e	7. i	8. a	9. c / h	10. f

Quiz 7

1. a	2. c	3. d	4. b	5. c
6. b	7. c	8. b	9. c	10. a

Quiz 8

1. b	2. a	3. b	4. c	5. d
6. c	7. b	8. c	9. a	10. b

Quiz 9

1.	c	2.	a	3.	c	4.	b	5.	d
6.	c	7.	b	8.	a	9.	c	10.	d

Quiz 10

1.	c	2.	d	3.	a	4.	c	5.	c
6.	b	7.	a	8.	d	9.	b	10.	c

PART FOUR

FINAL EXAM

BASED ON CHAPTERS 1–14

Name: _____ Date: _____ Section: _____

Directions: *Select the answer that best completes each statement.*

_____ 1. When you study, focusing your attention means

    (a) spending an entire evening on one subject.

    (b) not taking any breaks until you have finished all of your work.

    (c) setting goals and time limits for yourself.

    (d) studying at different times during the day.

_____ 2. Learning style refers to

    (a) how well a person comprehends the material.

    (b) how quickly a person learns.

    (c) the way a person learns.

    (d) how much a person remembers.

Directions: *Using context clues, select the best meaning for the italicized word.*

_____ 3. The lawyer tried to confuse the jury by bringing in facts that weren't *pertinent* to the case.

    (a) reasonable

    (b) continuous

    (c) relevant

    (d) harmful

_____ 4. Little Jill hid shyly behind her mother when she met new people, yet her brother Matthew was very *gregarious*.

    (a) insulting

    (b) sociable

    (c) concerned

    (d) embarrassed

_____ 5. Although most members of the class agreed with the instructor's evaluation of the film, several strongly *objected*.

    (a) agreed

    (b) debated

    (c) obliterated

    (d) disagreed

6. The noise in the nursery school was *incessant*; the crying, yelling, and laughing never stopped.

    (a) careless

    (b) harmful

    (c) bold

    (d) continuous

7. Dogs, cats, parakeets, and other *sociable* pets can provide senior citizens with companionship.

    (a) weak

    (b) friendly

    (c) dangerous

    (d) unattractive

8. Freshmen are often *naïve* about college at first, but by their second semester they are usually quite sophisticated in the ways of their new school.

    (a) innocent

    (b) sociable

    (c) annoyed

    (d) concerned

9. People who suffer from migraine headaches are frequently advised to avoid things that can *precipitate* an attack, such as chocolate and some cheeses.

    (a) prevent

    (b) trigger

    (c) follow

    (d) delay

10. When several members of the president's staff were charged with various crimes, the public's confidence in the government *eroded*.

    (a) grew

    (b) broke down

    (c) healed

    (d) repeated

Directions: *From the list below, select the proper word part so that the appropriate word is formed.*

(a) se   (b) terr   (c) trans   (d) uni   (e) vis

(f) phobia   (g) therm   (h) un   (i) ver   (j) voc

_____ 11. Fortunately, the vase was still _____broken after it fell off the shelf.

_____ 12. Can you en_____ion what you will be doing five years from now?

_____ 13. Since Tim conquered his acro_____, he no longer is afraid to climb ladders.

_____ 14. The photographs provided _____ification that Christy had indeed won the race.

_____ 15. It was difficult to find Rick because all the men were wearing _____forms.

_____ 16. The _____ain was obviously too rocky for either farming or grazing.

_____ 17. The minister's in_____ation began in the chapel service.

_____ 18. I decided to _____plant the bush to a different location.

_____ 19. _____odynamics deals with the relationships between heat and the mechanical energy of work.

_____ 20. Andy longed for the _____clusion of his farm after experiencing the hustle and bustle of the city.

Directions: *Select the answer that best completes each statement.*

_____ 21. The transition words "because" and "consequently" indicate that the writer is showing

     (a) a cause-effect relationship between two or more things or events.

     (b) each idea in order of importance.

     (c) how the previous idea is different from what follows.

     (d) how the previous idea is similar to what follows.

_____ 22. To imply an idea means to

     (a) reason out an idea based on what has been stated.

     (b) suggest an idea but not state it directly.

     (c) create connections between ideas.

     (d) provide support for an idea.

_____ 23. Paraphrasing a paragraph involves all of the following *except*

     (a) rewording using synonyms.

     (b) rearranging the order of ideas.

     (c) including your opinions and reactions.

     (d) maintaining the author's focus and emphasis.

_____ 24. The etymology of a word is its

    (a) pronunciation.

    (b) synonym.

    (c) history.

    (d) part of speech.

_____ 25. The best clue to identifying the topic of a paragraph is

    (a) the arrangement of the sentences.

    (b) the use of transitional words.

    (c) a frequently repeated key word.

    (d) the order of the details.

_____ 26. When evaluating an article's accuracy, it is important to verify its

    (a) generalizations.

    (b) style.

    (c) inferences.

    (d) source.

_____ 27. A writer who presents a one-sided view of a subject is said to be

    (a) critical.

    (b) objective.

    (c) biased.

    (d) factual.

_____ 28. The sentence that is a slanted statement is

    (a) In Seattle it rains six months out of the year.

    (b) There are nine planets rotating around the sun.

    (c) People who own pets live longer lives.

    (d) Television is the cause of all violence in schools around the country.

_____ 29. The sentence that is a value judgment is

    (a) Parents who have children should not get divorced.

    (b) Test scores in schools have decreased over the years.

    (c) Many elderly people can benefit by owning a pet.

    (d) Violence in the news may desensitize people to violence in real life situations.

_____ 30. An effective way to react to an author's ideas in a chapter is to

    (a) summarize the chapter.

    (b) create an outline.

    (c) make notes in the margin.

    (d) create a map.

_____ 31. As compared to major details, minor supporting details are typically

    (a) more general.

    (b) the same.

    (c) more important.

    (d) more specific.

_____ 32. Mapping involves

    (a) summarizing information in a chapter.

    (b) creating an outline from the chapter.

    (c) drawing diagrams to show how ideas in a chapter are related.

    (d) numbering ideas in order of importance.

_____ 33. A word's connotative meaning is its

    (a) exact dictionary meaning.

    (b) synonym.

    (c) implied meaning.

    (d) literal meaning.

_____ 34. Language that makes sense on an imaginative level but not on a factual level is called

    (a) figurative language.

    (b) connotative language.

    (c) denotative language.

    (d) literal language.

_____ 35. Objective language is language that

    (a) expresses attitudes and feelings.

    (b) is factual.

    (c) expresses an author's tone.

    (b) is persuasive.

Directions: *From the list below, choose the tone of each statement.*

       (a) instructive

       (b) persuasive

       (c) humorous

       (d) nostalgic

_____ 36. He never met a donut he didn't like.

_____ 37. Lock all the doors when you leave.

_____ 38. Every Thanksgiving, I fondly remember all my family gathered around the table at my grandmother's house.

_____ 39. Cosmetic companies should not be allowed to test their products on defenseless animals, all for the sake of making humans "beautiful."

Directions: *Select the answer that best completes each statement.*

_____ 40. The sentence which is an example of subjective language is

       (a) Cable television has brought many changes to the industry.

       (b) Children are exposed to more than a thousand hours of television before they enter kindergarten.

       (c) Greedy television producers and sponsors must start taking responsibility for the programs they are producing.

       (d) There are many reasons why our society is so changing.

_____ 41. In a textbook the preface typically contains

       (a) a list of vocabulary words.

       (b) charts and graphs.

       (c) the author's introduction to the text.

       (d) a list of the book's chapters.

_____ 42. Typographical aids include

       (a) italic type.

       (b) maps.

       (c) photographs.

       (d) charts.

_____ 43. When reading technical writing, you should plan to do all of the following *except*

       (a) read the material more slowly and carefully than other textbooks.

       (b) record important information in your own words.

       (c) reread and review various sections several times.

       (d) highlight all facts and details.

_____ 44. Textbook discussion questions are best for helping a student prepare for

    (a) vocabulary tests.

    (b) key terms used in the text.

    (c) essay exams.

    (d) important terminology.

_____ 45. A pie chart illustrates

    (a) how a process or procedure works.

    (b) causes and effects.

    (c) how parts of a unit have been divided or classified.

    (d) a comparison of events over time.

_____ 46. When reading a graphic, what is being summarized or illustrated can be found in the

    (a) key.

    (b) title.

    (c) legend.

    (d) footnote.

_____ 47. The graphic that could be best used to demonstrate height increases in boys between the ages of two and ten is

    (a) a pie chart.

    (b) a line graph.

    (c) an organizational chart.

    (d) a flowchart.

_____ 48. To find the main idea of a passage, first identify its

    (a) supporting details.

    (b) topic.

    (c) tone.

    (d) source.

Directions: _Select the one sentence that does not support the key idea presented in each statement._

_____ 49. Smoking is no longer as acceptable in our society as it once was.

    (a) Smoking has been banned on commercial airline flights.

    (b) A woman in Southern California was refused a job because she smokes.

    (c) Smoking is not permitted in many restaurants.

    (d) Using drugs has also become less socially acceptable.

_____ 50. There is good reason to believe that vitamin C can help prevent colds or make them less severe.

    (a) Studies have proven that people who take vitamin C catch fewer colds per year than others.

    (b) Studies have shown that the colds the vitamin C group catches last a shorter time.

    (c) Some scientists also believe that vitamin C can help prevent certain types of cancer.

    (d) Vitamin C reduces the severity of colds in studies done by scientists.

ANSWER KEY
Final Exam

1. ç	2. c	3. c	4. b	5. d
6. d	7. b	8. a	9. b	10. b
11. h	12. e	13. f	14. i	15. d
16. b	17. j	18. c	19. g	20. a
21. a	22. b	23. c	24. c	25. c
26. d	27. c	28. d	29. a	30. c
31. d	32. c	33. c	34. a	35. b
36. c	37. a	38. d	39. b	40. c
41. c	42. a	43. d	44. c	45. c
46. b	47. b	48. b	49. d	50. c

BIBLIOGRAPHY

Michael R. Solomon and Elnora W. Stuart, *Marketing: Real People, Real Choices*, 2nd edition. Upper Saddle River NJ: Prentice Hall, 2000, pp. 99, 107, 130-131, 429

Roy A. Cook, Laura J. Yale, and Joseph J. Marqua, *Tourism: The Business of Travel*. Upper Saddle River NJ: Prentice Hall, 1999, pp. 81, 127, 164, 253-255

Edward F. Bergman and William H. Renwick, *Introduction to Geography: People, Places, and Environment*. Upper Saddle River NJ: Prentice Hall, 1999, pp. 15, 62, 83, 307-308

Rebecca J. Donatelle and Lorraine G. Davis, *Access to Health*, 6th edition. Boston: Allyn and Bacon, 2000, pp. 116, 228-229, 517-518

John A. Garraty and Mark C. Carnes, *The American Nation*, 10th edition. New York: Addison Wesley Longman, Inc., 2000, pp. 153, 329-330, 712

Hugh D. Barlow, *Criminal Justice in America*. Upper Saddle River NJ: Prentice Hall, 2000, p. 362

George C. Edwards III, Martin P. Wattenberg, and Robert L. Lineberry, *Government in America*, 9th edition. New York: Addison Wesley Longman, Inc., 2000, pp. 262-263, 501, 631-632

Palmira Brummett, Robert B. Edgar, Neil J. Hackett, George F. Jewsbury, Alastair M. Taylor, Nels M. Bailkey, Clyde J. Lewis, and T. Walter Wallbank, *Civilization Past & Present*, 9th edition. New York: Addison Wesley Longman, Inc., 2000, pp. 237-238

Joseph A. DeVito, *The Elements of Public Speaking*, 7th edition. New York: Addison Wesley Longman, Inc., 2000, pp. 273-274

Stephen M Kosslyn and Robin S. Rosenberg, *Psychology: The Brain, the Person, the World*. Boston: Allyn and Bacon, 2001, pp. 400-402

Paul Gregory, *Essentials of Economics*, 4th edition. New York: Addison Wesley Longman, Inc., 1999, p. 186

B. E. Pruitt and Jane J. Stein, *HealthStyles: Decisions for Living Well*, 2nd edition. Boston: Allyn and Bacon, 1999, p. 80